DISCONNECTED JOTTINGS

Sam Mummery was born in Fareham, Hampshire in 1947 and had an undistinguished education at Hilsea College in Oakley just outside Basingstoke, Hampshire. He had a yen to be a fighter pilot but was turned down due to poor eyesight. However, he would doubtless have failed in his quest in view of the fact he was then and now unable to count past ten without taking his shoes and socks off. His interest in aviation continued and he began gliding with The Boy Scouts and went on to become a gliding instructor and a member of the British Glider Aerobatic Team. A 30-year career with British Airways as cabin crew came to an end when he was diagnosed in 1997 with Parkinson's. In 2005 he had deep brain surgery, which gave him his life back. He is single and lives alone in Hampshire.

DISCONNECTED JOTTINGS

Sam Mummery

DISCONNECTED JOTTINGS

Olympia Publishers
London

www.olympiapublishers.com
OLYMPIA PAPERBACK EDITION

A CIP catalogue record for this title is
available from the British Library.

ISBN: 978-1-84897-225-4

This is a work of fiction.
Names, characters, places and incidents originate from the writer's
imagination. Any resemblance to actual persons, living or dead, is purely
coincidental.

First Published in 2012

Olympia Publishers
60 Cannon Street
London
EC4N 6NP

Printed in Great Britain

This book is dedicated to Pat Mummery, my Mum, who sadly will never read it. Once, no mean wordsmith herself, she is locked into a 10 second loop of memory by dementia, and although she is happy and comfortable in a home, intellectually, she has left us.

Foreword

OK then, forward it is, not much point in going backwards because there is not a great deal to read until you get to this bit. The following will I hope provoke a smile or two. It is the accumulation of several years of scribbling none of which has been published before so my only claim to fame is a cheque from the editor of Canal and Riverboat just before the magazine went bust for the short story Butties Cuts and Stern Glands. Paid, but never published rare or what?

Bodgit and Scarper, and Fleesum, Grabbit and Runne are well-known firms to avoid at all costs. I wish I could claim to have invented them but alas that accolade lies elsewhere. However, the incidents, which appear in their correspondence, did not need a great deal of change to push them into the realms of fiction.

A straw poll of a few potential purchasers of this volume surprised me and also saved me from having to put in copious technical notes in explanation so I hope that the Alternative Bronze C Exam Paper will amuse those of you who have never needed to know what a katabatic cold front is, and may not know or care now or in the future.

I happily plead guilty to the charge of plagiarism regarding Pooh Bear but it is in admiration of A.A. Milne's style I salute his genius and compared with what Disney has done to the characters...

Some of the content will be very obscure so some explanation is required. ALOMA is translated as 'A Lady of My Acquaintance'. All the references to competitions are gliding competitions held variously in this country and abroad.

Lasham Gliding Centre, where I have been a member for 30 years is probably the world's biggest gliding site, with over 600 members. I have attached notes where the technical input may be a little daunting for the reader.

Acknowledgements

My thanks to Laurence Burgess for sorting the raw A4 manuscript into something resembling a book, free of charge, and my sister Liz Cory for re-typing the whole thing on my computer thus introducing me to a use for email which had eluded me until now.

Also my thanks go to Piers Bois, extraordinarily talented cartoonist and fellow gliding enthusiast who, over a very wet weekend in Jersey, designed the cover of the book you are holding, my only contribution was to ask if he could cram just one more character into the scene and to drink gallons of tea brewed by his wife Caroline and daughter Lizzy.

Sam Mummery
Bramley
October 14, 2010

Almost anyone can be an author, the business is to collect money and fame from this state of being.

A. A. Milne

CONTENTS

POEMS

SILENT FLIGHT

UNRELIABLE ADVICE

LETTERS – REAL AND IMAGINED

APOLOGIES TO A.A. MILNE

SHORT STORIES

APOLOGIES TO WORDSWORTH

Upon finding all the thermals full of gliders.

I grovelled trying to find a cloud
To lift me high o'er vales and strips
When all at once I saw a crowd
Of gleaming plastic superships
Beside the start line, above the trees
Lazily circling in not much more than a knot and a half I should think.

Continuous as the stars that shine
And twinkle on the Milky Way
They stretched in never-ending line
(And some were quite some way away)
Some twenty saw I at a glance
But I bet there were more than that, it was a damn big gaggle.

The standard ships were there but they
Outdid the short wing spans with glee
I looked aloft in some dismay
In such exalted company
I gazed and gazed and then I thought
I'm Damned if I'm joining that lot, it looks bloody hairy!

For oft when in a field I lie
Far from home and late in day
They flash upon that inward eye
I'll sell the house to help me pay
For a Nimbus 4Turbo with a glide angle too flat to plot and
Lots of instruments that go beep wee buzz beep beep and hot and
Cold ballast and a cocktail bar…

NOTES:
one knot rate of climb=approx 100 feet per minute.
Gaggle: collective noun. for gliders circling in a thermal.
Standard ships: 15metre wingspan.
Nimbus 4Turbo: Open class sailplane with 'get you home' capability.

DREADFUL DIRGE

It's been a long time since I wrote you a rhyme,
Credibility lying in tatters,
So I pen you this poem (1) in the hope that you're home,
So I now raise a delicate matter.

I'm back from Amurca on Thursday at seven,
And I hope we've a date around twilight.
Forgive my presumption, if I make the assumption
That you will still be around come the daylight. (2)

> (1) If you would indulge me in pronouncing poem as 'pome'
>   that would help quite a bit.
> (2) Please stay if you can.

"What do you think Eeyore," said Pooh.
"Drivel – complete drivel," replied Eeyore who was having a
particularly verbose day.
"I like it" said Piglet.
"OK," said Sam. Better send it and keep our fingers crossed.

So he did.

Just one of a series of dreadful dirges written for a lady of my
acquaintance (ALOMA).

LATE BIRTHDAY CARD

Roses are red
And cabbage is green
I know this is late
But I have just been
To Hong Kong and I didn't
Get back 'til Saturday morning
And it's not the sort of thing
You can ask someone else to post
'Cos they ask all sorts of awkward
Questions... so I hope you will
Forgive my tardiness... and I can't
Sign it either because it's supposed
To be anonymous... so I hope you know
Who sent it...
Help me somebody... I've got drivel overload
Heeeelp...

Written for a lady of my acquaintance (ALOMA).

WORDS COUNT

I read a couple of Sagas to her.
"Have you written one?" she asked.
"I've tried," I said, "It's very difficult."
"Does it have to be exactly 50 words?"
"Exactly," I replied.
"Write one for me."
"I'll try."
Later, at forty-seven, I needed three.
"I love you" fitted just perfectly.

January 18, 2004

This relates to the BBC Saga series where you are required to produce a 50 word story, which must include a beginning, middle and end.

AT THE END OF THE DAY

At the end of the day
And within your own style
If you feel where we are is on cue
Then building on this
And touching on that
You'll know where we're coming from too.

We do take your point
About Bristol and such
And we won't pass the buck on Penzance
It isn't the feedback we value so much
As the interested look in your glance.

When questions are open
The bar appears closed
And we'll test understanding on this
A somnambulant person appears to have dozed
It may be the wine with the fish.

Whilst pursuing a worthwhile achievable goal
We'll determine a realistic state
We'll stay on the target
Not sugar the pill
I'm gob struck. Are you the same mate?

Well moving on now
Really, how interesting
We'll cover it later, I'm sure
And pick up on that
Within your comfort zone
Which reminds me, my bum's rather sore.

It's appropriate now
At this moment in time
To discuss in the frank open manner

The use of this tool kit
We've filled all this week
Now where's that Pygmalion spanner?

In summary then
Now we know where we are
And we know what to do
And with whom
If you find the word interface
Creeping in here
We'll send Alistair back to his room.

You can see the course value perception is high
And the teams really know where they're at
Then praise Alistair, Lucy and Robert and Clive
And we'd all like to say
Thanks for that!

Thursday March 26, 1987

This is pretty well incomprehensible to anyone on the course, let alone the casual reader who wasn't. This is a gentle Mickey take on the British Airways Cabin Service Director's (CSD) promotion course, it contains all the buzz words current at the time, which is why I wrote it...

STUDLEY PRIORY

CYNICS
STOMPERS
STUDS

STUDLEY PRIORY HOTEL LIMITED   HORTON-CUM-STUDLEY   OXFORD OX9 1AZ
Telephone Stanton St. John (086 735) 203 & 254   Telex 23152 (attn. Studley Priory)

SOMETHING ELSE ENTIRELY

From unnatural acts to self discipline
And a smack of political smile.
I can't see a thing for the clouds and the rain
Which seem to be stretching for miles.

The use of the personal pronoun, and
Remember it's programme, not course.
From beating yourself with a hammer
To drawing a reindeer – not horse.

The grey man has felt that he's mixed up
But with Ps and with Ds makes a stand.
If we have an occasional minute
We could polish a cloud; that looks grand.

As we sit knee to knee here in silence
While you tell me nothing at all.
I'll just gaze in your eyes and admire you
'Til I fall off my seat on the floor.

It's Paris, so must be the spring
Depending on how you interpret,
Your rampant ambition assumes the condition
That fantasy's part of your remit.

The cause of the racket you're hearing
(Committed or not it's still there)
Is a load of sharp sand from Genghis & Co
Every grain is hand picked, very rare.

If your self-esteem drops to zero
And you're last to be picked don't despair
Kevin's I.Q's less than Gazza
And Trevor has lost all his hair.

Another British Airways (BA) programme. No tree hugging but plenty of cloud polishing. This is probably even more incomprehensible than the last one. Translations are available via the author at £20 a time.

Breakthrough August 1994

SNIP SNIP

He thought about it day and night,
Told his friends when he was tight,
Rocketing prices, children's gear,
Swept away last trace of fear.

To the clinic, in the door,
Shocked the nurses to the core,
Laid him on the theatre table,
He kept as calm as he was able.

Application of a needle,
Suddenly he's feeling feeble,
Snip snip and now the job is done,
Less fuss than if he'd cut his thumb.

Home at last and feeling cocky,
Wearing shorts by the name of jockey,
Feeling chirpy as a sparrow,
'Cept his balls are in a barrow.

Can't remember this guy's name but he looked after the Amiri Flight in
London. We took the Mickey unmercifully.

January 16, 1980

DUSIT THANI

Get booted and spurred
For a party I've heard
Is hap'ning in room five eleven
You can bring lots of wine
Or some beer will do fine
Just be there! – The time? Around seven*.

Concerning your clothing
We won't look with loathing
If you've left your gold lame in Luton
Just pull on some gear
You need have no fear
We're going to have fun... Rootin' tootin'!!!

*Actually anytime after six is fine. I just couldn't get it to
rhyme...

For the non-poetic this means Room 511 after six, spurs are optional.

Standard crew invitation to a party in the Dusit Thani hotel in Bangkok. No
further recollection of this day...

May 25, 1994

FOR GILLI AND JO

Tall and tanned and young and legless
Gilli stewardess weaving by
Knickers safely in her handbag
Showing yards of silken thigh.

Similar in most departments
(It's possible the hair has changed)
Enamel mug instead of handbag
Jo's a little more deranged.

Party games are what they're good at
(And other things not mentioned here)
One's a board game name of Pass Out
All you need are crew and beer.

When it's nearly turned two thirty
And you think you're thru' the worst
Jo knows places in Australia
Haven't closed since June the first.

If you doubt this ode is truthful
I can vouch for every line
Try a thirteen day with these two
They'll have you on your back in nine.

Went down with tonsillitis halfway through this 13-day trip but after two
days in bed in Perth Australia I was back with them.

MISS YOU? CORSE NOT!!!...

Except once or twice, well, seventy-nine times if you want to be picky; when I wanted a hug. Waking up in the middle of the night wondering what you were doing. Mind you I put that down to the fish and chips, which I'd eaten earlier.

I will admit to a couple of occasions when we were parked next to a Qantas jumbo I had the oddest feeling that you'd been in it.

Just in passing I should like to mention the day in Los Angeles. Whilst gazing at the Pacific it occurred to me that if I dipped my hand in the water and by some chance you just happened to be testing the water temperature in Sydney Harbour then at least we would be touching the same ocean, albeit ten thousand miles apart.

I was having a kind of warm feeling about that when some ill-mannered relation of Jonathon L. Seagull dived out of the sun and nicked a huge chunk of my ice cream (vanilla with chocolate sauce), which I bought only because I needed some comfort food you understand... Anyway, I got this mad idea that he might fly across to Sydney and present it to you, and as I was pondering how very romantic that would be, the rest of the ice cream fell out of the cone and a squadron of J. L. Seagulls caught it before it hit the water, thus preventing delivery to you by the benign tides and currents of the aforesaid body of water.

Perhaps worth mentioning, if you are still interested, is the return trip.

A gin clear night, pitch-black sky and towns and cities visible hundreds of miles away.

The cabin is quiet, most of our four hundred charges are asleep. I'm sitting in the cockpit and we are all watching the Northern Lights; they are weaving and shimmering, painting the sky in silver, blue and green. Nobody speaks, there is no need to say how beautiful it is. I want to share this with you and I miss you lots...

A touch of the miseries in LA.
The more enlightened of you will notice that this clearly isn't a poem but I didn't know where else to put it.

SILENT FLIGHT

Aerobatics Proposed Regulation Implementation and Limits
Phase 1
Le Guerre De Derriere
Wings of Season (Whinge in Season)
Competitions Directors Reports 2007, 2008, 2009
The Serenity of Silent Flight
Problem Page
The Alternative Bronze C Paper
The Santa Interview
Hockenheim August 1989

AEROBATICS: PROPOSED REGULATION, IMPLIMENTATION & LIMITS

Phase One

For some time now concern has been expressed that aerobatic flights operating within the airfield perimeter may come into conflict with other gliding operations.

We propose, therefore to run a trial beginning today which should separate aerobatic and ab initio training and also local and cross-country soaring.

A box, the dimensions of which are shown on the plan below, will be activated from 600 to 4500 feet QFE, in which only aerobatic flight will be permitted. To facilitate this initiative the following operational changes will be implemented.

WINCH LAUNCHING

A launch window 150 metres and 2000 feet high will be opened to allow winching from the main runway. On release pilots must observe the box restrictions by flying to the nearest point outside the box *without circling.*

AEROTOWING

Tug pilots have been briefed to remain below 600 feet QFE until they are outside the box when they may climb normally.

CIRCUITS

Clearly circuit planning will be of vital importance under these new conditions.
It is recommended that the downwind leg is omitted and approaches are flown directly on to the base leg aiming to arrive at the edge of the box at around 500 feet. To avoid conflict gliders with registrations containing vowels should fly a left hand circuit and those with consonants a right.

If today's trial is as success we hope to make it a permanent feature so your co-operation and constructive criticism will be appreciated.

This caused such consternation when I put it on the notice board at Lasham that we had to remove it in the interests of air safety. If it hasn't clicked yet, try reading the title line again.

QFE is an altimeter setting height, it refers to height above an airfield as opposed to above sea level.

April 1, 1996

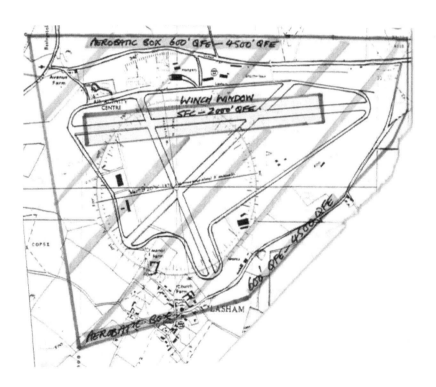

LE GUERRE DE DERRIERE

The battle for the bottom line continued today amid wide speculation that the American, John (Red Arse) Mahony is planning a spectacular coup for the second unknown compulsory.

His half snap on a vertical downline in the free programme which created a storm of indifference amongst the judges is likely to be eclipsed by the half snap on a horizontal line, though sources close to the organisation do not think that the score will vary much.

Meanwhile Sam (I wish my glider was not so distinctive) Mummery has consolidated the position he established in the first known compulsory where he produced a rarely exhibited display of unity amongst the judges for five of the eleven figures.

The contest Director later described the performance as one of the funniest he had seen for years.

STOP PRESS

The Commonwealth Drinking Team having established an early lead while the Australian member was present has continued to improve its performance since the addition of Mahony as an honorary member.

The word around Venlos' bars is that at the final on Saturday next, the team will produce perfect rolls on a downline and score well at horizontal figures towards the end of the evening.

World Glider Aerobatic Competition Venlo, Holland 22/8/93.

We finished within a couple of points of each other.

"WINGS OF SEASON"

By

William Brian Wark

Glistening white wings of summer
Lift me through the purple haze of
Late July
Let me drink the cooling mist
Of cloudbase
And visit secret places in the sky.

In this single moment be my transport
To shining heights where only eagles
Cry
That I might breathe this lightning
Blue of mid-year
And hold the bank with steady hand and eye.
Embrace the lightest nudge of stick or rudder
To keep the fickle yaw string flowing
True and
Share the deepening joy that climbs
Within me
Among these feathered streets of blazing hue.

For surely it will not always be summer
Quite soon the gray of autumn winds
Will blow
And bend too hard against the spars
That hold me
Besetting skills and loves gained long ago.

The distant firelight of spring is waning
And only dreams of flight too soon
I'll know and
The steady touch which this day smoothes the
Turning
Will tremble with December's crusting snow.

So glistening white wings of summer
I beg you promise
When that darkening winter night for me
Draws nigh
That you'll one last time lift me
Beneath the heavens
To that place where great thermals and
Old pilots go to die.

WHINGE IN SEASON

by
CYNICAL B'STARD

Grubby fly blown wings of K8
Pissing rain and eight eighths murk
Standing drenched outside the hangar
Feeling like a bloody berk.

At this moment can't get transport
To shining heights where eagles cry
So I'll wade across the mud pond
To change my socks which once were dry.

Heave the stick and kick the rudder
It doesn't matter what I do,
The bloody yaw string's going sideways
Stuck to some bird shit, just like glue.

Surely this cannot be summer
With icy wind and lashing rain
Soaking through the ply and fabric
Failing glue and splitting grain.

The distant crash of thunder waning
I dream of launching heaven bound
Forty-seven in the winch queue
Cable foul up, driver drowned.

Stuff your glistening wings of summer
Sod the purple haze, and prose,
Open up the bar my handsome
Let's get bloody comatose.

'Wings in Season' appeared on the notice board at Lasham during a competition. I didn't meet the gentleman concerned but put this up next to it and the following morning it had disappeared. No sense of humour – the Yanks.

DIRECTORS REPORT 2007

Thursday morning, a slate grey sky and a forecast which seems to indicate that the gods are not at all pleased with our intention to paint the sky with beautiful lines and angles. While the rest of Britain basks in warm sunshine Saltby lies under a thick layer of murk, which begins at around six hundred feet. I scrub at three o'clock, thunderstorms are threatened.

Friday. Cloud lifts and so do spirits until Lionel Sole reports from a tug that "there is no horizon and it's like flying around in a milk bottle". He does not indicate if it is green or red top... The Unlimited pilots decide they don't like it regardless of colour. I scrub again, am I destined to be the only director in 15 years to fail to have a contest at the Nationals?

Saturday. Despite the forecast it looks promising. I climb into the motor glider with CFI. Les Merrit, still no horizon and a 1500 ft cloud base but it's improving. We split the unlimited known and Andy Cunningham flies it from 2500v feet – the rest follow. By the time the Intermediate are through their split program we have nearly 4000 ft between the ground and the fluffy stuff. I begin to think we might just do it The Judging position is swiftly changed so that the sun is behind the judges, thus ensuring that they can see what they are scoring. By 17.00 we have a competition with two programmes flown in Unlimited. Can we get everybody one flight so we can declare a champion in all classes? Despite a sea breeze front which brings a line of cloud through the box lowering the visibility and a commercial balloon lurking to the east of the field which defies our attempts to communicate, by 20.45 it's in the bag. A magnificent job by all concerned.

Sunday the slate roof returns, Brief at 9.00 and decide a firm cut off time of 13.00. Scrub at 12.55 followed by the glittering prizes.

Note: Jim Duthie is the best damn launch point controller in the universe...

Saltby is renowned for its interesting weather, as these three reports will bear witness.

THE GLIDER NATIONAL AEROBATIC CHAMPIONSHIPS – 2008

It is a fact universally acknowledged, at least by the aviation orientated, that Saltby can produce some of the most capricious conditions one is likely to encounter where aviators forgather. And so it was for day 1 of the 2008 Glider Nationals. With a record entry of 24 pilots we really did have a challenge on our hands.

The cloud base remained stubbornly static until the afternoon when the sun broke through and allowed a split programme albeit with some irritating delays to allow patches of rogue cumulus to pass through the box. Thanks to the co-operative spirit which is always about at the Nationals, getting the aircraft onto the launch grid before briefing reaped dividends and Jim Duthie in his 15th and last year as launch point controller ensured that pilots were strapped into the correct glider and in the right order, no mean feat with 10 pilots sharing the same K21. We will miss you Jim.

Congratulations to the new National Unlimited Champion Mike Newman, Paul Barker who took the honours in the first glider advanced contest in the UK. Brenden O'Brien in the Intermediate, Matt Plumridge, Sports, and the three beginners with Jonny Mak just pipping Emeric Massaut by 0.23% with John Firth in third place. Their scores of 77.31% 77.08% and 75.23%... remarkable standard or what?

My thanks to all at Saltby led by the irrepressibly cheerful Les Merritt, to the judges and their scribes, and to the competitors. Now where do I find a launch point controller who can move cu-nims to one side by will power...?

SALTBY OPEN 2008

"Bother," said Pooh, "It's raining."

"That," commented Eeyore gloomily, "is a masterpiece of understatement. It is, to be more precise coming down faster than a no frills 737 with a pressurization problem. The precipitation is most persistent; it is, to use the vernacular, pissing down."

"Thank you for your valuable contribution Eeyore," said Pooh with heavy sarcasm.

"Don't mention it," replied Eeyore. "Hardly anybody does so I don't expect it anymore."

"Expect what?" asked Pooh who had been distracted by a glider bobbing about in a large pool of brown water just outside the Saltby clubhouse.

"That is exactly what I mean," mumbled Eeyore "No one listens, nobody cares," and he stumped out into the rain.

A moist Piglet arrived. What was left of the colour in his striped T-shirt, which he had worn every day for some 70 years, had drained from the garment and it was now a grubby cross between mould and dry rot.

"Very smart," cried Tigger who wasn't supposed to be in this piece at all, but evidently had let himself in with a spare key. "When do we fly? Can I get a launch?"

"You'll be lucky," said Eeyore. "The contest direct and the chief judge have just taken the last one. They were last seen sailing in the direction of Grantham."

THE SALTBY OPEN GLIDER AEROBATICS MEETING 2009

I am not, as regular readers, both of them, will confirm very complimentary about the general weather picture at Saltby, having presided over one complete washout and several truncated contests... so the drive up the A1(M) on the day before the Open in bright sunshine was a pleasant surprise. I was even more surprised to watch the cloud, which hung at 1,500 ft climb and disappear by about 11 a.m.

So by opening time we were very much ahead of the game. Far enough ahead to have a discussion about what we were going to do to keep the pilots amused having completed the contest flights well before lunch on the second day. And so the 'Funfree' was born. There were some interesting programmes, the most original of which was Graham Saw's, with a performance consisting entirely of rolling circles which, for reasons I can't recall, was not scored by the judges.

Prize-giving took place with His Grace the Duke of Rutland, an active member of Saltby doing the honours, ahead of a barbeque, which was well attended, and of the usual high standard.

Thank you to all at Saltby for your enthusiasm and hard work.

A selection of my better director's reports from competitions at Saltby where the British Nationals are held each year.

THE SERENITY OF SILENT FLIGHT

(A realists guide to Glider Aerobatics)

1. It is not generally appreciated that before you can "slip the surly bonds of earth" you have to remove your aircraft from its box and put it together. This will require the assistance of up to four willing helpers who will rapidly turn into one not so willing helper as soon as they have assessed the weight of the wings... "cos I did my back in the last time I lifted one of those..."

2. Prior to stunning the judges with a breathtaking performance you will be required to fly in formation (line astern) for up to 20 minutes behind a pilot who is dreaming of commanding a large multi engined jet transport and is not always completely familiar with the minutiae of height, positioning and drift as it effects your machine.

3. A glider has a rate of deceleration on a vertical upline, which will surprise you.

4. It also achieves a rate of acceleration on a vertical downline, which will terrify you.

5. Gliders are not silent. The noise emitted by a metal glider when subjected to load can be disturbing particularly if you have never sat inside a dustbin while it is being beaten by an enthusiastic percussionist equipped with a baseball bat.

6. Item 5 notwithstanding, your howls of invective when spinning off a stall turn, may quite possibly be heard by the judges and perhaps influence their scoring; although up to now no evidence exists of penalties for profanity.

7. Stall turns are impossible in gliders. (This is a personal statement and I do not wish to discuss it further.)

8. You are required to land "expeditiously" after your sequence. If you have drifted out of the competition box and that last figure

used a bit more sky than intended you may find that your landing becomes more expeditious than planned. Try to pick a field with an uphill slope and don't forget to thank the landowner. Avoid cows; they regard gliders as a tasty snack.

9.   When examining your score sheets do not react hastily to the judges' comments. If your perfect four point roll has been described as "off line, soft hesitation and dished" patiently and quietly locate their car and let all the tyres down...

10. Nobody EVER scores 10.

August 1999.

THE PROBLEM PAGE BY ALBATROSS

Dear Albatross,

I took up gliding some eight months ago and the effect has been shattering.

My wife left me after I re-mortgaged the house to buy a glider, my boss has threatened me with dismissal if I have to leave the office for any more 'sudden funerals' and I spend large portions of the summer months staring at the sky and mumbling in an incoherent manner. What should I do?

Albatross replies:

You say that all this has happened in just eight months. This is really quite remarkable progress. You will soon be able to class yourself as a truly dedicated glider pilot.

You should now plan to move up the scale on equipment. As you have already re-mortgaged you should investigate alternative ways of raising the necessary capital. Selling your children into slavery is but one option you might consider.

As far as your boss is considered, a more flexible approach is required. Recurring bouts of malaria on good soaring days are difficult to disprove and can be used at very short notice. You do not state your age but you might also consider shrapnel movement from an old war wound as a standby.

I trust your progress will continue.

Dear Albatross,

After flying I like to enjoy a Bloody Mary in the bar. On several occasions lately I have experienced a sharp pain in my right eye whilst enjoying my post soaring beverage. Could this discomfort be related to altitude or cross-country fatigue?

Albatross replies:

I doubt it, try removing the swizzle stick *before* drinking.

Dear Albatross,

My boyfriend is not keen on gliding (his abiding love is the study of Natterjack Toads). On the rare occasions when he has accompanied me to Lasham he always confronts me on our relationship just as I am about to take a launch. This usually takes the form of, "Well Pricilla, it's either the glider or me." What should the answer be?

Albatross replies:

"Take up slack..."

THE ALTERNATIVE BRONZE 'C' PAPER

1. The 'Angle of Attack' is...

A. The blind spot which prevented you from dodging your syndicate partners' fists after you landed with the wheel up.
B. A carefully prepared but badly researched complaint concerning waiting lists.
C. A K8 coming straight at you in *your* thermal.

2. What do you understand by the letters Va?

A. An abbreviation for a London museum.
B. An incomprehensible algebraic form.
C. Nothing.

3. Induced drag is...

A. A lecture on katabolic cold fronts by the most boring member in the club.
B. Getting your foot caught in a winch cable whilst it is being retrieved.
C. Being persuaded to wear a dress at the Christmas lunch.

4. 'Stonking' describes a thermal strength of...

A. 5 Knots.
B. 8 Knots.
C. Off the bloody clock, I couldn't believe it, must have been pulling trees out of the ground etc. etc.

5. The strength of thermals and speed of a task flown (when not supported by documentary evidence) is in direct and inverse proportion to the skill of the pilot telling the story.

A. True.
B. Too true.

6. How long does a 'five-minute' gliding job take?

A. 1 hour 7 minutes.
B. 2 hours fifteen minutes.
C. I'm sorry, I'd like to help but I have to collect my daughter from the dentist.

7. When standing with your back to the bar (in the northern hemisphere) on which side will the C.F.I. accept a drink for completion of a silver distance?

A. Your left.
B. Your right.
C. Either side if there's a drink in it.

8. The minimum requirement for winch driving at Lasham is...

A. Commercial pilots licence with instrument rating.
B. Airline transport pilots licence with 6000 hours and fly by wire experience.
C. A high boredom threshold.

9. The correct weak link for a glider is determined by matching the colour of the link with the colour of...

A. The pilots' fingernails.
B. The wingtip holders' eyes.
C. Any instructors eyes after spin training.

10. When rigging a glider, grease should be applied as follows...

A. To the rigging pins and then to the trousers.
B. To the fingers, rigging pins and trousers.
C. Nobody ever has any grease when you need it.

11. You land your glider on the lawn of a large and stately home in Southern England. What is the correct form of address to the landowner?

A. Sorry old man, had to drop the old kite onto your green sward, simply dying for a jimmy riddle.
B. Wotcha cock, you got a smart drum 'ere John 'ent 'cher? Any danger of a big gin then?

C. If you'll call off the lions, Sir, I'm sure we can come to an amicable arrangement about the damage.

12. This question for instructors only.
What should you do when asked to mark a Bronze C paper?

A. Feign deafness or senility or both.
B. Direct the student to a brand new assistant instructor whom you dislike.
C. Attempt to mark it and then resign your rating.

For 'Rising Air' 17/May/92

The Bronze 'C' is an early step in the Federation Aviation International (FAI) badge system for glider pilots.

THE SANTA INTERVIEW

It took several months to arrange and, predictably, security was tight; Mr. Claus guards his privacy closely and since this was the first time he had granted an interview to anyone, I was not surprised to be asked to don a blindfold as I was led to the waiting aircraft, the modern mode of transport to Santa's Grotto.

What followed, however, was not so much a surprise as a revelation.

I had always supposed that the Man in Red inhabited an isolated area not far from the North Pole. Imagine then my amazement when, after a flight of some eight hours, I was led, blinking, into bright sunlight and a temperature of plus twenty-nine degrees centigrade.

My minder, a large man of few words, was kind enough to exchange my fur lined Parka and moon boots for a T-shirt and Bermuda shorts after which I was ushered to a waiting limo where the blindfold was once more applied.

Thirty minutes later I was relaxing in a leather armchair in the sitting room of a mansion, which was straight out of a Hollywood film set.

A middle-aged man struggled through the six inch pile of the appropriately, snow white carpet, his hair was bleached blonde and he wore a pink satin shirt open to the waist to reveal a very large gold medallion.

"Good trip son?" he enquired, extending a hand encrusted with a number of rings, which exhibited more extravagance than taste. "Not quite what you expected eh?" I agreed it wasn't, nor was the Cockney accent for that matter. "Media stereotyping is the problem," said Santa, for it was indeed he. "You wouldn't believe how conservative people are; don't like change, makes 'em nervous." There was no doubting the validity of his statement, I was feeling a shade nervous myself.

I composed myself, removed the little umbrella from the pineapple daiquiri, which had mysteriously appeared at my side, and posed my first question.

"When did you move to Florida?"

"'Bout five years ago; couldn't stand the bloody cold, you wouldn't believe what I was spending on heating and it's dark half the year; gets you down." I nodded.

"Besides," Santa continued, "we had to modernise, diversify, you know how it is, stuck out there in the middle of nowhere you lose touch with the market place."

"So in what ways have you changed the image?" I asked, "What about the elves, the Grotto, the reindeer and sleigh?"

"Oh we still got the elves," said Santa flicking a piece of tinsel off his shoulder. "Don't call them elves any more though; vertically challenged is the correct term. Anyway they formed a co-operative some time ago. Call them Santa's Helpers and Integrated Trades. Got the Toys-R-Us franchise sewn up."

I winced. "And the reindeer?" I said, hardly daring to ask.

"Had to let them go, got to be a liability, 'specially Rudolf. You know the song about the shiny nose?" I nodded. "You don't know the half of it son; pissed as a pudding most of the time, no wonder his bloody nose was red. I remember one Christmas Eve he tried to slow roll the sleigh right over the top of Milton Keynes at 800 feet. Shook me up I can tell you, presents all over the shop. Then next thing I know I'm getting letters from the C.A.A, it couldn't go on. And talking of the C.A.A., nigh on impossible to get a permit to fly a sleigh these days, something about the width of the runners, and airspace problems; well I don't have to tell you..."

He didn't.

"How do you get around these days?" I asked, anxious to leave the subject of airspace in case anybody was listening.

"Always leave the best 'til last," said Santa, getting to his feet.

"Come this way."

He led me to the smoked glass patio doors, which slid open as we approached with a barely audible hiss. At the bottom of a lavish garden stretched, to my astonishment, a wide ribbon of tarmac. Poised gracefully at its threshold and gleaming in the sun was a glider.

"Schempp Hirth and Schleichers* got together and built it for me," said Santa, "solar powered, self launcher, G.P.S., the works." He ran a hand over the glistening curve of the nose. "Got a couple of unusual features" he continued, "I've replaced the stick with a pair of reigns and got hold of some sledge runners instead of a wheel; well you got to hold on to some tradition haven't you?..."

* Schempp Hirth and Schleichers are well-known German glider manufacturers.

HOCKENHEIM AUGUST 1989

This Death has a brother, swift, violent and devastating.

I will never forget the sound, the crack of a twig amplified until it seemed to split the sky and the crackle of the fabric as the slipstream tore it off the wing. We watched transfixed. silent but for one voice "Get out! Get out!" And we watched as the wing now a sycamore leaf in autumn revolved slowly in the afternoon sunlight. A moment etched into time as lady luck withdrew her patronage and left the stage.

The once graceful lines of the sailplane were gone. No longer a creature of the air, fatally wounded and unable to respond to the guiding hands of its pilot, gravity wrenched it from the sky and flung it to earth; terra firma claimed its prize. The next sound that hot afternoon was the sound of Christof dying.

Doing what he loved to do, doing what we all loved to do.

And tomorrow we would do what we loved to do again and defy the monster we all pretend does not exist.

April 26, 1989 – A memory remembered by a poem about death.

This came out of the blue when I was taking part in a speedwriting competition where one takes words at random from a book and constructs a story. It brought it all back to me as described. The glider broke up recovering from a stall turn and Christoff was unable to bail out in time. The KOBUZ 3 glider which the Poles had at that time flown exclusively was grounded from that day.

UNRELIABLE ADVICE

Today is the beginning of your journey down the adult highway.
The trials and tribulations you have experienced up to now are but nothing
to the challenges ahead.

Here is some vital intelligence to help you on your way.

1. Batteries always fail when the shops are shut.
2. Cars do not run forever on one tank of fuel.
3. *You* always have to put fuel in the car.
4. *She* always has to put fuel in the car
5. Women like flowers and phone calls.
6. Women do not like late, pissed, amorous men (however, as a general rule they will tolerate them since there are so few of the on-time, sober variety about).
7. If you still have the shiny black wrapper from your brand new golf ball in your pocket, you will hit your next shot into the water.
8. No woman has successfully grasped the offside law in Rugby Football.
9. Banks exist to sell you money, which is fine except that their prices make Harrods look like a village hall bring and buy sale.
10. Traffic lights are programmed to remain red for twice as long as normal if you are late.
11. The well-documented sexual performance level provided by four pints of Guinness, one bottle of Claret and two Cognacs is largely a myth.
12. Merchant Bankers make a lot of money.

Enjoy the party Brad.

July 11, 1996 Bradley Shore – University Graduation.

WOT IS THIS THING CALLED, LUV?

A guide to boats and boating equipment for the new sailor
Compiled by "Fender Man"

As you will very soon discover, boats have a lot of bits, most of them attached to other bits with a variety of materials. Whoops! For instance the particular bit you have just tripped over is a Headsail Sheet Winch. Yes, I bet it did hurt; it's made of steel...

As I was saying, there are lots of them and they all have confusing names. This is to enable people like me to behave in a patronising manner when you confuse a halyard (pronounced hal- ee- ard) with a fairlead (pronounced "quite a long way ahead") though how any confusion arises is beyond me; they are not remotely alike.

But I digress. The following notes on many aspects of boating may enhance your enjoyment of the experience. Mind you, it might not, of course, so if that is the case I apologise in advance.

CATAMARAN. A twin hulled vessel popular because of its generous accommodation and the fact that it does not heel over, thus reducing the potential gin and wine spillage by a considerable margin. Rule one for this craft. Always ensure that both hulls, or pontoons, as they are also known, are pointing in the same direction before sailing.

ROPES. N.B. There are no ropes on a boat, once on board they become LINES. When used to *raise* or *lower* a SAIL (explanation later) the line becomes a HALYARD. Conversely a line used to *control* a sail is a SHEET. Lines also become WARPS and SPRINGS from time to time.
So that's all clear then, we'll move on...

SAIL. A very large piece of material which is attached by one of its edges to a very long stick, placed vertically in roughly the middle of the boat. Its lower edge is attached to another stick, which is itself attached to the first stick I mentioned earlier, but in the horizontal plane of course, and can rotate about the vertical stick through 180 degrees if left unsecured. Ask an experienced crew member to explain the rules of "Boom butting" a challenging game where players are knocked out one by one until the last player shouts "wearzakin manesheet?" indicating the end of the game.

KNOTS. Apart from the bowline the tying of which always provokes enthusiastic dialogue wherever the nautically inclined forgather, the hearty exchanges on methodology involving various animal species exiting holes and circling trees before diving down their holes again. The resultant knit wear has been known to turn heads at W.I. Sales nationwide. The only knot which you really need to master was made famous by Sir Francis Chichester when he used it to effect a temporary repair on a rotary clothes drier in the back garden of a holiday cottage in Devon during one of the great storms of the 80s.

It is of course the Running Overhand Reverse Becket Hitch. Your Captain will be delighted to demonstrate its many uses.

PORT & STARBOARD. (Left and Right)

Here is an easy way to remember which is which.

"Darling, have you seen the Tailors Late Vintage?"

"Have a look in the Dresser sweetie."

"Right Oh, my love."

"Can't see it, precious."

"Perhaps it has all been consumed, poppet."

"That's probably why they left early, my only love."

"What, just because there was no **port left**? What a bunch of creeps."

I'm not too sure it's supposed to go on that long but you get the idea.

A FEW GENERAL HINTS

Be tactful with any foreign crews you may meet, especially the French and Spanish. Their forebears got a right stuffing from one "Horatio Lord Admiral Nelson" in the early 1800s and find it difficult to reconcile their defeat with a sailor who was careless enough to lose an eye and an arm in previous unpleasantness. References to Trafalgar should be restricted to navigation.

It is a serious breach of etiquette to use the Red Ensign, or indeed any countries' national flag as a beach towel regardless of its similarity to the ones you got in Tenerife last year.

If you take on the task of Kitty Master you will be expected to look after money for the rest of the crew and also check the size of narrow navigable inlets with a cat (as in "not enough room to swing a cat"). Cat swinging is a risky and demanding discipline and should not be undertaken lightly. Those of you who intend using the existing ship's cat instead of bringing your own placid moggy are warned to take adequate precautions.

Walking the plank and keelhauling have largely disappeared from commercial cruising these days but there are just a few boat skippers who hanker for the days when men were men etc.

The most notorious of these is undeniably **"Wild dog" Wulford** who masquerades as a quietly spoken Airline Captain on holiday.

It is only when at sea his true character is revealed and his excesses when "in drink" are as varied as they are shocking and have no place in this epistle.

He may give himself away though, you should watch for these signs.

He insists that the boat be moored and all gear secured by opening time (when in the U.K) and by dusk elsewhere to ensure that his alcohol levels remain high, and will become visibly distressed if these timings are questioned. He dislikes cold weather; a drop in temperature of only a few degrees will find him going below to "check the navigation". It is reported that he has scuttled to the chart table whilst still in the marina at Portsmouth. And finally, if you find a perfectly made hangman's noose dangling from the topping lift early in the morning you are in for an interesting day...

SAM MUMMERY
March 5, 1996

BREAKFAST

My marmalade's called Nigel
And my toast is called Elaine
I bet my butter wishes
That it had a proper name

"I wish," said Butter "nothing of the sort, and I resent the implication that my name is somehow improper."

She gleamed a rich gold in indignation.

"I'll have you know," she continued, "that my family background is impeccable. No preservatives here – pure and natural is what you get with me. Not like that Elaine, or whatever she calls herself now," she added. "Wasn't called Elaine when she was just a piece of bread was she? And from a sliced load, too. Gets in the toaster for a bit of a tan and then starts putting on airs and graces. She'll wind up a stale old maid, you mark my words." She paused in order to control a minor melt resulting from the passion of her verbal outburst.

"I have always preferred muffins myself," she murmured. "Much more rounded personality altogether."

"And as for 'Nigel Marmalade' – doesn't exactly roll off the tongue does it? I hear his parents were Silver Shreds not The Coopers Oxford thick cut he claims, except possibly the thick part, which fits admirably in my opinion. Now you will have to excuse me while I get between them or heaven knows what trouble they will cause on the breakfast table..."

January 30, 1994

ALPHABET FOR OUR TIME

A is for Asbo and hoodies and stuff
B is for Bankers, enough is enough
C is for credit, tricky to find
D is for debit the very last line
E is for excess and no rules expenses... to clearing Moat and repairing the fences...
F for fantastic the lies that they told
G is for Gordon and the gold that he sold
H is for Hansard where the story unfolds
I is for me, all for me I believe
J is for justice, which some don't receive
K is for killing fields, wax jackets abound and like the green wellies are fashionably sound
L is for lifestyle, lavish of course, the name is Lavinia, and she looks like her horse
M is for money it's a difficult time so the gin and tonic comes with lemon not lime
N is for nationality lottery of birth. Simpler to say "Citizen: Planet Earth"
O is for Order, as in out of and Speakers
P is for politics whistle blowers and leakers
Q describes a line that's unique to Britain
Don't try to push in you'll be labelled a cretin
R is for racist and the phrase that betrays them, "I'm not racist BUT"... then comes the mayhem.
S is for sex not the act but the gender
T for temgesic after a bender
U for University and the glittering prizes
V is for vapour in various guises
W is for Women in all sorts of sizes
X is for Xylophone a difficult instrument
Y is for Yangtze, where the Brits had an incident
Z is for zither and zeal and zoom also for zit and zoology Alas and alack I haven't got room to discuss Zebra biology.

May 20, 2009

SINAH WARREN

Sinah Warren... A sequel to Watership Down perhaps? But no, located on Hayling Island in Hampshire it used to be a Holiday Camp. Only the term 'camp' has been dropped in favour of 'village'; thus removing any hint of internment. I have to admit that my first impressions were not encouraging.

I have never been very comfortable with "are we having fun yet?" venues and we were but 20 PD and carers among the 600 strong group. However, the staff were friendly, the rooms spacious and comfortable, the food excellent and plentiful and all the areas of the Warren were wheelchair accessible.

Given the above and convivial company the answer to the question was, yes, I think we are (having fun that is... do try to keep up).

My introduction to Bingo was a sobering experience. How do people cope with three blocks of numbers? I was still searching for two fat ladies when we were well past legs eleven. Monty Gatehouse, who is good with figures, called a line or a shed or something and won fifty quid! My respect for bingo players everywhere is now well established.

I regrettably remained a spectator for the line-dancing, since I am acutely aware that dancing of any kind inevitably results in both myself and anyone foolish enough to partner me ending up flat on our faces amidst wreckage of tables and drinks. However, the rest of the team were up for it and very good they were too. Have you ever tried a Californian left traverse shuffle? You should...

Friday's cabaret was excellent with the staff, who all appeared to be multi-talented, doing a 'Cities of the World' routine in song and dance with breathtakingly swift costume changes. The high standard continued on Saturday with the very funny Bradley Walsh, of Coronation Street fame.

Did I mention Rabbit Racing? No? Well, until you have attempted to haul in a wooden rabbit on a length of string which is threaded though your legs and attached to said rabbit **behind** you – well, look, you had to be there...

My rabbit was called 'Inalight White-Winesauce'. Well, it's a bit more original than 'Stu'.

Sunday morning dawned bright and frosty so off I went to sample the historic delights of Long Bow. Yup, you got it, Archery. Managed to get all three of my arrows away without taking anyone's eye out, but also failed to hit the target with one of them. They do go a long way in free flight... The last I saw of it was when it disappeared into a clump of nettles, some twenty yards behind the target. The instructor, whose day had obviously not started well, was not amused. I thought it wise to quit the field to avoid any unpleasantness.

Sunday night cabaret featured a Lulu look-alike whose voice was very much like the real thing. Her last number, which must be obligatory for this sort of tribute, the big hit 'Shout' rocked the rafters, great stuff.

And that as they say was that. I had a great time and I think the rest of the team did too. The whole thing was beautifully organised by Gill Dunn, a lady of boundless energy whom I have no doubt is planning our next trip as I write this. By the way, did you know that many of the voices for the Thunderbirds puppets were done by Bob Monkhouse? Nor did we which is why we scored 19 out of 20 on the Sunday night quiz...

March 04, 1996

THE GEORGE & DRAGON INSTANT EXPERT GUIDE NUMBER 16

THE PLANET EARTH

The Earth is where we live. It is round and is a long way from the moon. It is even further away from the sun especially during February in Cleethorpes.

Because it is round, Planet Earth has a diameter and a circumference. If you know what the diameter is you are a precocious little bugger aren't you? But you can also work out which is the shorter route to the other side.

It says in two very big books wot I found that the diameter of the Earth is 12,756 Kilometres. Which is a nasty foreign measurement brought in by asylum seekers together with beri beri, social unrest and terminal athletes foot. So I have changed it to nice comfortable British miles.

So the diameter is 6883.1 nautical miles and different if you measure it with statues apparently. I don't have any statues handy so we will use the sailors measure.

If you multiply this number by pye, which today is chicken and leek, or to express this numerically 3.14159 recurring (I don't know ask Simon, he does numbers) you get 21,623. It is therefore clear that the shorter route is the diameter. Unfortunately this route involves a great deal of time consuming tunnelling so the round the houses, and indeed round practically anything you care to mention, option would appear to be favourite.

9 April 1994

SELECT HOUSEHOLD ARTISANS GUILD

Dear Phil

Congratulations on your career Diversification.

At your age your courageous move into the domestic labour market may present a number of challenges. Here at **S.H.A.G.** hope that the following may assist you to meet the demands of your newly chosen discipline.

The attached Starter Kit contains the basics but it is up to you to breathe life into these inanimate objects.

Note carefully, the following advice:

1. Guard your Marigolds jealously, they are your badge of rank, NEVER lend them to anyone.
2. You should always be able to quote accurate figures regarding the 'extra' dishes which may be cleaned when using various types of liquid. (Miss Nanette Newman is a world authority on the subject and her bestseller 'Sweegy Bottles I Have Known and Loved' may be of use.)
3. When negotiating your first position as a Household Artisan ensure that service standards are not compromised. When interviewing perspective employers the phrases 'I don't do brass or wynders' should be introduced at an early stage.
4. Replacement of the essential equipment in your bucket is the responsibility of the employer but it must be made clear from the outset that anything within this container is for your exclusive use and that any modification of the location of the vessel (traditionally in the cupboard under the stairs) must be the subject of full consultation between the parties involved.
5. Straightening of pictures moved in the normal course of dusting is not your responsibility.
6. Whilst in the working environment the eyes should never be raised further than the horizontal. Dust or cobwebs accidentally observed above eye level should be ignored.

7. Remuneration should always be 'up front' and in cash; remember our proud motto NON PECUNIA NUMERATA, NON MUNDO (No cash, no clean). We wish you every success in your new venture.

Sincerely yours

A.Leydee-Waatduzz
Gen Secretary S.H.A.G.

For Phil Wharton. Presented with bucket and cleaning materials at the G&D March 13, 1996 after he voluntarily washed up the previous Saturday for 3 hours.

BATTERIES NOT INCLUDED

It will not have escaped your notice, and if it has, then the following may be something of a revelation, that advertisers are currently indulging themselves in an orgy of what I am pleased to call "honesty" messages to would be consumers. These little snippets appear at the bottom of the TV screen, are very difficult to read and do not stay long, they invariably begin with "Terms and conditions apply" and list some of them, although you would have to be a speed reader of considerable skill to digest the content.

Banks are particularly good at pulling the wool, with a great many "New customers only" messages. One can fully understand why a customer of some twenty years might be somewhat brassed off to find that the spotty adolescent ahead of him is getting a better deal than the careful, prudent and conservative Mr. Average. What price loyalty? £100 apparently – since a large banking group are offering that sum to new customers but terms and conditions apply here too. One of which is that you must have £1000 minimum in your current account. I wonder if that includes the gift or not.

I don't know whether the phrase "some assembly required" originally described MFI's infamous flatpacks, those three words are guaranteed to strike fear into the hearts of otherwise competent adults. I have a friend who is convinced that their demise, MFI's that is, was hastened by losing control of the number of screws supplied to each customer. He tells me that every pack left him with between four and eight screws and up to three pieces of bent metal for which he could find no location... If you multiply these figures by the millions of units sold he might have a point, however, my experience and a straw poll of a few friends and neighbours seemed to confirm my assertion that there were more holes than screws and I don't recall any bits of metal bent or otherwise. But I digress, anything with SAR in its advertising or on the box it came in should immediately be passed to a child of not more than seven years who will be at the peak of his or her skills having just completed a Blue Peter course on the construction of box girder bridges *Disconnected Jottings* using only the cardboard centres of lavatory paper rolls and sticky back plastic. (Yes I know that the correct name is Fablon but the company folded 2 years ago.) The BBC have been stockpiling the stuff for decades. If there is a resurgence of bad taste in the fitted kitchen market they could really clean up. I have I fear strayed from the point which was the essentially dishonest manner in which the bad news on any deal is covered up. At least with the small print one had time to get out the specs and magnifying glass to find that the beautiful villa you booked in the middle of nowhere is hosting a Star Trekers' seminar for 500: 300 of whom are attempting to emulate Captain Jean-Luc Picard with varying degrees of success. The remainder posing as aliens of evil intent etc. And if you had not ignored the very last page having located an electron beam microscope to enable you to read it you would have found a reference to these events happening throughout the summer.

Five-year warranty on cars should be treated with grave suspicion. You will probably be locked into a contract, which requires you to use a manufacturers garage and their outrageously overpriced parts, £381 for a piece of plastic wheel and sill trim for a popular Japanese saloon for example. These prices will of course not protect you from the embarrassment of finding that you cannot stop the vehicle because of a fault in the system for which umpteen thousand vehicles are being recalled.

To return to banks for a moment, a new service providing very short term loans of up to £1000 is now advertising and stating that this service should not be used for long term financial planning; I should hope not with an interest rate of 2600%. No that's not a typo. Two thousand six hundred percent... In fairness I have to say that they are very upfront with the rate, it comes up on the screen in big figures and stays there long enough for everyone to gasp and scream outrageous! They should be locked up etc, etc.

The only way to make sure that you have read these messages of course is to record them. Thus making us the only country in Europe who record advertisements instead of programmes, mind you given the quality of the material these days... Oh and you may well have seen the latest bit of nonsense added at the end of any advert for alcohol "Please enjoy Let's get Legless Lager responsibly".

August 12, 2010

FINE THANKS, AND YOU?

I confess to finding myself in a bit of a quandary; how to convey to an enquirer that I may look great but I actually feel decidedly second hand "How are you?"

"Fine thanks," I say, even when I feel and look, if not actually at death's door, certainly adjacent to it.

The point about this whole thing is that "HOW ARE YOU?" is not an enquiry about you or your health, nor is, "How do you do?" They are, of course, forms of greeting.

"How do you do?" probably came into fashion during the plague years when hearing someone say they were fine didn't quite cut the mustard, in view of the fact that people suffering from a mild case of acne or the odd cold sore were avoided like the, er – plague.

There are those who are of course unable to observe the social niceties when confronted with this question. They feel obliged to answer honestly. I have some sympathy with this view, if I feel awful why does convention prevent me from saying so. Why should it be out of order to describe in detailed and colourful prose a gall bladder operation which got complicated, then really dodgy, and was finally sorted out by a team of consultants. I'll tell you why it is out of order, because nobody is in the least bit interested in the medical experiences of anyone but themselves. So, how to respond without clearing the room faster than a gentleman in a tea towel waving an AK47 and screaming "death to all infidels" but nevertheless indicating that you are not at your best.

Any attempt at modifying the response, such as "not so bad, mustn't grumble" is doomed to failure, as is "well if you complain nobody listens, so what's the point?" Anything that suggests that you are going to give a measured and serious reply: "since you ask, my back has been playing up something cruel for weeks now..." Just watch the expression on their faces, benevolence to boredom in a millisecond.

You could try to excite curiosity with "excellent thanks taking everything into consideration", this coupled with a weary smile indicating the brave struggle you have been coping with so admirably.

How about "much better now thanks" adding "compared to last week" to ensure a further enquiry about your condition during the last seven days.

Or, "I shall know more when the test results are in..." It helps if you can recall at least one of the tests and what it was for, beware of mentioning "specimens" or the difficulty of filling containers with same... Adopt an air of detached resignation, "hey ho we shall see".

Of course the phrase is so embedded in the greeting there is a good chance that whatever you say in reply will not be heard at all. "How am I? Ghastly thank you, I very much doubt if I shall make it to the end of the week." To which you will in all probability receive the hearty reply, "Excellent, and you look good too..."

January 18, 2009

I think I may have offended a few people with this one. It is, however, based on years of experience...

NATIONAL GEOGRAPHIC

NATIONAL GEOGRAPHIC

1145 17th Street N.W., Washington, D.C. 20036-4688 U.S.A.

JOHN GRIFFIN
Executive Vice President
President, Magazine Group

THIS IS YOUR
FINAL NOTICE.

Dear Member,

Unless we receive your renewal instructions immediately, your name will be dropped from the National Geographic Society membership rolls.

Even though you have missed the delivery deadline for two NATIONAL GEOGRAPHICS, you still have time to reinstate your membership.

But you must do so immediately because we will not be able to send you another reminder.

Just return the enclosed Renewal Form with your remittance. It couldn't be easier. Thank you.

Sincerely,

John Riff

P.S.   Think how much your family members gain from NATIONAL GEOGRAPHIC's blend of information, imagination, and insight. Renew now for them—as well as for yourself.

John Griffin
Executive Vice President
National Geographic
1145 17th Street NW
Washington
D.C. 20036-4688
USA

2nd April 2004

Dear Mr. Griffin,

I had hoped to slip away unnoticed, fade into the background, drift out of sight; I should have known better of course. And now I face the ignominy of a FINAL NOTICE and if that were not damning enough, it comes from the lofty eyrie of the Executive Vice President, Magazine Group, no less. Well, not exactly from you personally, now I come to examine it more closely. It has the look and feel of having been generated by a machine and I'm addressed as "Member". I must, I suppose accept this anonymity. Quite soon now, my name will be dropped from the National Geographic Society membership rolls. I have been warned.

I imagine this to be a ceremony similar to being cashiered; my name ripped from the ancient parchment, my metaphorical sword broken in two and the pieces thrown to the ground at my feet. I must admit I sensed a cloak of shame beginning to envelope me, despite the fact that my good friend and confidant, Charlie "Two Chins" Fanshaw, is of the opinion that someone will merely select "delete" on a computer screen – somewhere in the depths of 1145 17th street, and that will be that. Charlie tends to be a bit of a pragmatist on these occasions. Thirty years as an "S" bend checker in the sanitary ware industry has dealt a severe blow to his romantic side and lately he does tend to see things in black and white, or to be accurate, white and brushed pampas, very popular colours for bathroom suites in the 80s I understand.

Forgive me, I have strayed, somewhat, from the point.

My chastisement continues in the next two paragraphs and then, immediately below what purports to be your signature, the Post Script, a masterpiece of innuendo and implication. "OK you moron we can do no more for you but at least have the decency to save your children from the swamp of ignorance in which you insist on wallowing," it screams.

I do not feel it appropriate to describe in detail the sudden demise of my entire family in a tragic and bizarre encounter with a flock of Rutland Ridgebacks, as you may be aware, a particularly aggressive breed of sheep, since my analyst is at one with the very widely held view that I imagined the whole thing. Nevertheless your assertion that I have a family is breathtakingly presumptive.

In conclusion you might ponder, before allowing your name to be attached to such a crass document, why I no longer wish to subscribe to your magazine. If only you had just asked.

Yours Sincerely.
Sam Mummery

No Reply!

BODGIT AND SCARPER (UK) LTD.
MISCELLANEOUS WORKS DIVISION
(OUR MOTTO IS TO SERVE YOU RIGHT)

CARAVAN TO THE LEFT OF KEBAB VAN
LAST LAYBY BEFORE M5 TURN OFF
GLOUCESTERSHIRE
TEL: WE REGRET, TEMPORARILY NOT RECEIVING
INCOMING CALLS

9th August 2001

Dear Madam,

I regret to inform you that a number of serious breaches of our Company Code of Conduct occurred whilst our employee Mr Mummery was engaged in essential maintenance to your dwelling yesterday and the day before.

His eccentric behaviour is of great concern to us in the Building Industry where a traditionally slipshod attitude to workmanship has been nurtured over many years.

As a woman, of course you cannot be expected to appreciate the wider picture and the likely consequences of Mummery's extraordinary attitude to the job.

I would like now to list his shortcomings so that you may be able to grasp the reasons for our disquiet in this matter.

1. In blatant disregard of established practice he apparently, arrived **on time.** You will no doubt appreciate that punctuality in the industry could lead to jobs being completed on schedule, which also implies that they might also be within budget, the result of which could be the loss of thousands of jobs within the Banking and legal professions.

2. Having to some small degree made up for breach number one by taking a coffee and lunch break 'back to back' thus ensuring that not a stroke was done before two o'clock, he allegedly spent **three and a half hours** on an electrical installation, a task which clearly cried out for the services of an Emergency Technician and Safety Assistant, on the astonishing pretext that he was determined not to be beaten by an inanimate object. I put it to you dear lady that if we all carried on like this we would have a recession of Biblical proportions on our hands.

3. We now come to the ultimate betrayal of long established practices, which have served to keep the members of this industry in jobs, which under less enlightened leadership would no longer exist.

On the second day he completed two further electrical installations without the previously mentioned Emergency Technician and Safety Assistant. Not content with this heresy he accepted assistance from **YOU!!!**

I can only imagine that you must have been overcome by some sort of fantasy about doing a man's job. I'm sure I don't have to spell out the consequences of this dangerous dalliance. It could easily lead to equality of the sexes, women in dungarees and feminine hygiene products on open sale in the workplace. Could any greater catastrophe overtake our closed and cosy world? I think not.

To conclude, there is a strong rumour that this loathsome creature actually resecured a hosepipe to a wall despite the fact that it had not fallen off. His reason for this? Because although secure he did not think it was a particularly good job!

This is however, such a fantastic story that I am prepared to accept that it is the product of a fertile imagination and intend to set it to one side. We have of course terminated Mummery's contract but regret to have to inform you that he is rumoured to be setting up on his own.

I urge you most earnestly to have nothing to do with him should this be the case.

You are of course assured of **our** very best traditional services when the need arises, or at least within 14 working days (not *Disconnected Jottings* 66 including Saturdays or Bank Holidays) of that time subject to availability of staff and materials plus VAT.

Yours sincerely
I Bodgit
Non Executive Director and not really involved financially since you ask Officer.

FLEESUM GRABBIT AND RUNNE
SOLICITING DONE, OATHS COMMISSIONED

27 August 1971

Dear

My client, Mr Sam Mummery, finds himself, once again, in need of our services to rectify a number of breaches of etiquette which he feels may have occurred on the night of Saturday 25th August and early morning of 26th August 2001, at a fringe entertainment arranged by your good self, as part of the Upton Water Festival.

As a preliminary he apologies unreservedly for his loud and crass remarks suggesting that there was a lot more sodding water about in February when he had to take a 25 mile diversion to get anywhere near the town, and there was no mention of a festival then.

He realises that this may have caused offence to some of your guests who even now, are discovering mutant goldfish in their bidets and are still involved in the tedious process of ridding their cellars of marauding alligators.

He feels also, that he may have given more attention to the bare midriff of your daughter, than was entirely necessary or appropriate in a male of his age. With this in mind he deems it prudent to ask for 26 other cases involving other young ladies present, to be taken into consideration. Their names unfortunately escape him for the present.

In mitigation he suggests that Davina Clutterbuck may have misunderstood his request at an earlier location for, 'A small soft drink please', as: 'Slosh half a pint of Vin Ordinaire in there girl, I'm gasping'. This mistake is entirely understandable in view of Mr Mummery's previously observed alcohol consumption which, it has to be said, was not noted for its moderation.

Whilst the name Clutterbuck is fresh in your mind, it is possible that further breaches of good manners may have been initiated by an incident, which occurred 'offsite', on the return from the (excellent) fireworks display.

Whilst recalling the night she was deflowered in the back of a Capri 2.3 GLS in Burnished Gold with Black and Mauve Luxury Suedette Trim (the Capri was in burnished gold, not Mrs Clutterbuck) she had occasion to chastise a fellow motorist for a minor lapse of courtesy which she achieved by opening the passenger window and uttering the words, 'Hey you tosser' in a most strident manner. Since my client was seated in the front seat, he felt obliged to undertake a minute examination of his left shoe, thus revealing a level of cowardice seldom seen in modern times and rendering him vulnerable to high levels of stress.

This incident was a catalyst, later on, for the unfortunate expression 'God Davina, that was great sex' which my client insists was used 'only as a joke' when he followed Mrs Smith from the front door of the 'Sympathetically Engineered Barn Conversion', leading to part grassed garden featuring authentic Caribbean Bar, Boule Park and Swimming Pool, following a longish chat concerning, amongst other things, objectivity.

Mr Mummery would like it noted that the reaction of Mr Cedric Smith to this lewd outburst was, 'Good on you Sam my boy!' A remark, which he hopes, may persuade you not to go ahead with your claim for damages.

Suffice it to state, finally, that my client 'had a lovely time, thank you' and lives in hope of once again being invited to share some time with your delightful family and friends. He is, however, unable to offer any guarantees that his behaviour in future will undergo any improvement.

Yours faithfully
Frank Fleesum

The names have been changed to protect the guilty.

FLOOD ALLEVIATION SCHEME

The Owner/ Occupier
23 LONGBRIDGE ROAD
TADLEY
RG265AN

Engineering

Ref.   **BB745691**
Name Matthew Thompson
Phone 0845 9200800

03 December 2007

Dear Customer

Bramley Foul Water Flood Alleviation Scheme

I am writing to up date you on the work we are undertaking in Bramley. As you are aware we are undertaking this work to alleviate foul water flooding to some properties in Bramley. We have been in discussion with Hampshire Highways regarding the diversion route and we are in the process, following their request, of ordering more signs, which will be erected as soon as they are available. Please note that there are **no diversion signs** in Bramley around Folly Lane, Oliver's Lane as these roads are not suitable for large vehicles or large volumes of traffic. We and Hampshire Highways wanted to keep through traffic away from the area and have therefore erected diversion signs on the A33 / A339 / A340. This is the official diversion route. However, please note that the small lanes are public highways and we cannot stop road users from using them. We can only continue to try and discourage people from using these roads as shortcuts. Furthermore we are intending to enhance the signing at the A33 and A340 in a further attempt to discourage through traffic to lessen the pressure on the local road network.

Residents have asked both ourselves and Hampshire Highways to consider implementing a one way system through Bramley. This has been considered carefully but it will have other safety implications for local residents and is not currently a preferred option. Following discussions with Hampshire Highways we have agreed to keep the road swept regularly by our Contractors, J Murphy and Sons. We will also carry out some reinstatement work in Folly Lane where the road is particularly uneven. They will also continue working as quickly as possible to minimise the disruption the road closure is causing. **Please note that when we return in the New Year, we will again close the Sherfield Road and this will be from 3 January 2008 to 1 March 2008.**

We have been in discussions with the local bus company and requested that they use the diversion routes that have been put in place. Although, we cannot enforce this, discussions will continue.

If you have any comments regarding this project please call our Customer Centre on 0845 9200 800 quoting your address and our reference number **BB745691**. The lines are always open.

Yours faithfully

Matthew Thompson
Project Communications Consultant

Thames Water
Clearwater Court
Vastern Road
Reading
RG1 8DB

Registered in England and Wales
No. 2366661, Registered office
Clearwater Court, Vastern Road,
Reading, Berks, RG1 8DB

Dear Mr Thompson,

If you find this letter offensive, then I shall feel the warm glow of success spreading through my body, the feeling that can only be experienced when one is sure that one has put down a "Consultant".

Yes, I am aware that you are undertaking work in Bramley, but only because my car is now covered in a protective coating of mud collected from the verges of the village where those of us with vehicles of reasonable size have to scamper to avoid the bullying tactics of hordes of Range Rovers, Jeeps and other 4-wheel drives, full to bursting with the progeny of Ruperts and Abigails, on the School run. This is of course not your fault, but I just wanted to get it off my chest.

It is a bloody shame that when you were "in discussion" with Hampshire Highways, it did not occur to anybody that it is not a good plan to erect signs which advise drivers that a road is not suitable for diverted traffic without giving some clue as to what is suitable. I wonder how you intend to enhance the signs on the A33, Fairy lights perhaps, a hanging basket or two, or better still a gibbet with a "Project Communications Consultant" strung up by his genitalia...

Mind you, your "strategy" (not a word with which you are familiar I imagine) in attempting to discourage through traffic has provided a boost to the bottom line of several pharmaceutical companies who specialise in stress related drugs. Watching the pathetic attempts of grown men attempting to grasp an instruction to use a diversion which cannot be identified because the manufacturers are still unable apparently to deliver "Road Closed" and "Diversion signs on time or it seems up to two weeks late, is distressing. Reports abound of over 60 cars in convoy trying to find a route to the A33. They had been trying for 3 days before abandoning the search as futile and rumour has it that they have set up a hippie type camp in Morgaston Wood and are surviving by ambushing Tesco delivery vans for food. I fear the worst...

Yours etc.

Gas and Water Mains plus flood relief work June to September 2008. Reply to Thames Water re-disruption during roadworks – July 08

BRITISH AEROBATICS ASSOCIATION

Ben Ellis
Chairman
British Aerobatic Association
19, Thistledene,
THAMES DITTON,
Surrey   KT7 0YH

Tel 020 8398 2114

e-mail Chairman@aerobatics.org.uk

Sam Mummery
23 Longbridge Road
 Bramley Tadley
Hants RG26 5AN

30 January 2005

Dear Sam,

We were discussing the matter of Who's Who in the Association recently when the subject of honorary membership came up. At once, several voices were raised saying 'what about Sam Mummery?'

Well, we then discussed the considerable effort that you have put in over the years, especially in getting the Aerobatic Glider Championships off the ground and the support you've given that cause. As a result, I'm delighted to say that we decided to confer on you the status of

Honorary Member of the British Aerobatic Association.

I hope that you are able to accept this position, with our thanks for everything that you have done.

With best regards,

Ben Ellis,
Chair,
British Aerobatic Association.

Registered Office: British Aerobatic Association Ltd., c/o West London Aero Club, White Waltham Airfield, MAIDENHEAD, Berkshire SL6 3NJ Registered in England No. 1168665   www.aerobatics.org.uk

Ben Ellis Chairman
British Aerobatic Association
19 Thistledene
Thames Ditton
Surrey KT7 0YH

27th Feb 2005

Please forgive the long delay in replying to your letter.

I've been having a rather trying time dealing with indecisive French doctors.

All is now sorted I'm very pleased to say and we leave for Grenoble on March 31st.

I'm extremely touched and not a little flattered to accept the position of Honorary Member of the British Aerobatic Association.

I'll do my best not to let it go to my head. Putting H.M.O.T.B.A.A. after my name won't fit on the stationery anyway, and since it could easily be confused with "Head Monitor Old Time Breakdancing Accident Audit" an organisation with which I have had a close relationship for some years. I will be careful that the two disciplines do not come into conflict...

In all seriousness, Ben, I am very proud to have been associated with Aerobatics and to have experienced the sheer joy of painting pictures in the sky, even when I was not entirely sure which end of the canvas I was supposed to be filling.

I hope to be back soon in order to continue my lifelong ambition, to have the stall turn eradicated from the Aresti catalogue...

Many thanks and regards to all.

* Adam*

CONFUCIUS HE SAY IT TIME FOR ORIENTAL KNEES-UP. PHIL & CAROLINE SAY IT JOLLY GOOD IDEA.

YOU COME WARSHASH SOON PLEASE AT SAT 31st MAY 2003. YOU COME IN EXOTIC COSTUME SO WE HAVE JAPANESE BEER CEROMONY. MUCH ORIENTAL FOOD TO BE EATING. CAROLINE HAVE BIRTHDAY TOO SO GOOD EXCUSE.. TOP SYMBOL MEAN RSVP. YOU COME PLEASE TO IMPERIAL PALACE 25 CROFTON WAY WARSHASH AT 8 O'CLOCK. AH SO.

IMPERIAL HIGHNESS CARRORINE 01489 581014 / CHAIRMAN PHULL 01425 478172

PHIL & CAROLINE REPLY TO PARTY INVITATION

19th May 2003

Gleetings Implelial .highness .Cawwowrine an Charman Firripp,

I have to hand your most onerable comoonick asian in which I note that the prolific sage and onion... bugger... sage and fillofficer Confusedus, better known, as I am sure her highness will confirm, as K'ung Fu-tzu, the Master K'ung, is still saying things despite suffering a terminal attack of death in 479 BC. (I hope you are impressed with this, it's all verifiable given a few books and time on your hands!)

He also had some pissy...solly, pithy remarks concerning female aerobatic pielots which I will relate at some other time.

It is with leglet that I am unable to attend your Oriental Knees in the up or even down and locked position, due to a plevious commitment to and Occidental event, namely Ihe Blitiss Airlobattick Chumpy on ships at Sortby in the county of Restassure or it may be Rinkonsure, but it is an area known as Estangria and involves many clazy person frying downside up in airopranes lacking any visible or audible means of support.

Enough of this nonsense, the bloody spill chocker is seeking psychiatric help and I don't do TiePiN!g

Solly I can't make it, and hope it goes well as I am sure it will given your track record.

Yaws sinseeree

THE BARQUE MALODOROUS

ON BOARD THE BARQUE "MALODOROUS" OFF THE COAST OF GOD KNOWS WHERE...

I have to hand this day your esteemed epistle to which I reply with as much dispatch as possible given the conditions at present prevailing. Due to an administration error of immense proportions Blind Pugh has been elevated to the position of NAVIGATOR.

He is, as I write attempting to feel his way across the ocean using something he calls Braille. This very morning we took a huge diversion around a piece of carrot cake, which the cabin boy failed to remove from the chart, need I say more?

However, to the business of the 19th day of August in the year of our Lord 2006 and celebrations attached thereto. I shall instruct my agents to secure any passage available to the island of Jersey on that day. Might I enquire as to the possibility that suitable lodgings may be available, my needs are modest (double, en suite, 24-hour room service, mini bar and trouser press). Is there perhaps an example of the popular franchised Admiral Benbow chain close by?

I note the dress code and have instructed my staff to locate a parrot (I favour a Norwegian Blue) so as to avoid the threat of plank walking, a sport at which I have never excelled.

I close in haste as this wretched vessel is, I am told, about to run aground on a spillage of Brown Windsor-soup...

I remain Madam your obedient servant

Reply to 50th Birthday and thank you letter. 1-8 Aug. 2006.

Admiral Benbow Cybercafe and Chinese Massage Skegness.

The "Malodorous" having run aground on a sandbank which the wretched Pugh failed to "Feel", I find myself in the care of the above establishments staff, a rum lot by any standards. And by any standard there is a lot of rum about, not to mention gin, whisky etc. The salvage team led by a Mr Silver are confident that they can refloat the vessel on the next tide and say they will deliver her to Portsmouth by the end of the month, all being well. They have advised me to remain here to sort out the inevitable paperwork. Mr Silver is an amiable gentleman despite his somewhat bizarre appearance, he has but one leg, the result apparently of the corrosive effect of years of parrot guano contamination. His lawyers, the well-known practice Messrs. Fleecem Grabbit and Runne assure me that he is a man of integrity and that I should place my trust in his organisation, Shoestring International Salvage. Must close as Pugh has found a pineapple which he is convinced is a Braille globe of the earth... Bye the bye lovely party thank you very much for having me. The enclosed are "Photographs" which haven't been invented yet so are really quite special. I think they may well catch on...

KANGA AND THE LOST NIGHT

Kanga opened her eyes, or at least she managed to open one eye and experienced a sharp pain behind it, which dissuaded her from any attempt to subject the other one to the same treatment.

A loud scraping noise invaded her world and turning her head, not without some difficulty since it appeared to have become larger and heavier then she recalled, managed to locate the source of her irritation. Roo, or someone who looked like Roo but had gone fuzzy round the edges was writing their name with a pencil on a piece of paper.

"Don't do that Roo dear," said Kanga; but it was not what she said at all. Regrettably it appeared that a person or persons unknown had without her knowledge or consent, installed a high quality shag pile carpet around her tongue while she slept.

The resultant "durr broo thaaa oooo raaaa" which was projected towards her noisy offspring was less effective in silencing his activities than it might have been.

Kanga turned her head again and at the same time accidentally opened the other eye, an action she immediately regretted as a searing pain tore across her forehead, accompanied by a stunning (in every sense of the word) array of coloured lights which on another occasion might have been quite entertaining.

Roo, sensing that something was amiss; the something being the fact that his mother had been replaced by a lurching red eyed hearthrug which emitted strange and threatening sounds; fled in search of Christopher Robin who, no doubt, would be able to make some sense of this bewildering metamorphosis.

"Good morning Kanga" said Eeyore cautiously. "I don't want to trouble you and heaven knows, a lot of people around here think that just passing the time of day..." Eeyore paused, and when he had finished pausing he started staring and staring, as everybody knows is not something that donkeys do on a regular basis.

"You don't look well," Eeyore said at last. "I'm not one to be unduly pessimistic but I am of the opinion, and it is only my opinion of course, which counts for very little round here. I am of the opinion, as I mentioned just now, that you might be dead."

"Not quite," replied Kanga through clenched teeth. Her relief at having reclaimed the power of speech was diluted somewhat by the reaction of a nearby previously evergreen bush, which when enveloped in her breath shed all its leaves and began a slow decline from which it would never recover.

Christopher Robin arrived and assessed the situation instantly, which was curious given his unconventional upbringing and lack of fashion sense (I mean to say; Clarke's sandals and bare feet at his age).

"Hello Kanga," he said softly. "I think these might help." He dropped two tablets into a glass of water. The sound they made, thought Kanga, was uncannily similar to being subjected to a depth charge attack.

"I take it Mary was here," said Christopher Robin, skilfully catching an empty bottle of Rioja as it rolled towards the edge of the coffee table.

Kanga nodded. "And I expect you phoned Pooh and insisted that he speak to her." Kanga nodded again. Further response did not seem necessary and nodding was less painful.

"Certainly did!" exclaimed Pooh heartily as he bounced through the door. Kanga thought she detected an air of superiority in his manner.

"Pissed as puddings, both of them. Positively paralytic. Patently plastered."

"I think you've made your point," murmured Kanga. "Now go away and let me die in peace."

"Ok," replied Pooh. "See you when you feel better," he added whilst harbouring an uncomfortable feeling that it would be unwise to milk this one for what it was worth.

And of course he didn't. "Mind you," said The Bear of Very Little Brain to himself. "I could have some fun with it from time to time..."

HKG, March 20, 2001

PAULA'S FALL

"As I understand it," said Christopher Robin, "Paula was doing some gardening when she fell off a box."

"How far up was it?" asked Pooh, who had been reading a book on Urban Plant Propagation.

"Not a window-box," said Christopher Robin "a box for standing on…"

"Or falling off," interrupted Piglet, who had just been on an adult literacy course and was getting tiresomely quick-witted. "Was she pissed?" enquired Piglet.

"Not at all," replied Christopher Robin, "but Lionel was when he realised he'd have to work Saturday night..."

Card to Paula Shore after she broke her foot.

PIGLET'S TIDY UP

"Well," said Piglet, "perhaps I do need a bit of a spruce up, but how am I supposed to make a decent job of it with this tatty old thing? I mean, just look at it. Hardly any bristles and the handle's bent."

"There is a very good reason for that," said Eeyore with as much gloom as he could muster.

"Is there?" said Piglet who had learnt that it was wise to be non-controversial when in conversation with Eeyore.

"Indeed there is," replied Eeyore with a note of triumph. "And that very good reason is," he continued in a tone which Piglet didn't care for very much. "The fact that the item to which you refer as a; and I quote; tatty old thing, is in fact my tail."

"Ahhh..." said Piglet. "Sorreeeeee."

THE TROUBLE WITH VALENTINES

"The trouble with trying to be a Valentine," said Pooh to anyone who was listening which on this occasion was Piglet... "the trouble is that with us not being anatomically correct..."

"Aunty Who?" said Piglet.

"Anatomically Correct," repeated Pooh. "It means that we are not in all respects complete as regards to the sort of bits required for the purpose of being a Valentine."

"Get away," said Piglet who had picked up the phrase from a television soap and had no idea what it meant.

Pooh gave Piglet a look which would have turned milk sour had there been any in the vicinity and then continued, "We are not for instance, in possession of hearts."

Piglet thought hard but failed to manage more than an "Oh" which was just as well since Pooh was, for him, bordering on verbosity.

"It will not have escaped your notice Piglet," Pooh continued "that we are filled with stuffing, or it may be stuffed with filling, I'm not sure exactly. But the fact remains that we do not have hearts and you will know if you have been paying any attention at all, Valentine's Day seems to be all about hearts."

"Christopher Robin says it's all bollocks," said Piglet.

Pooh looked at him. "That, Piglet, is an altogether more complex problem..."

February 14, 1993

GLOVES

"Have you ever tried to rhyme anything with GLOVES?" said Pooh.

"Not so that you would notice," replied Eeyore.

"But then even if I did, nobody would."

"Would what?" enquired Piglet.

"Notice," replied Eeyore, and he gave them a long gloomy look.

"Ahh," murmured Pooh and began a minute examination of the piece of paper he was holding.

"Tricky one Pooh?" asked Christopher Robin.

"Mmmmmm," mmmed Pooh. "Gloves rhymes with loves but you need something with it because it's a verb... It is a verb isn't it Christopher Robin?"

"I think so Pooh Bear," said C.R. "How about this... 'Pooh's got some gloves Which he loves But only because they're the gloves Of the one that he loves'."

"Pitiful," said Eeyore from the safety of the gorse bush.

"It's not for you, I think it will do and it's true," retorted Pooh.

"Now that is more like it," said Eeyore with something that sounded like mild enthusiasm."It almost scans; bit of work here and there..."

"Thank you Eeyore" said Pooh quietly. "I like it the way it was."

Hope you do too...

November 25, 1999

PARTY INVITATION

"Hmmm," said Eeyore. Except he didn't really SAY it, he more sort of... well, Hmmmed it as only Eeyore can if you know what I mean. "Hmmm. I don't like the look of that. In my not inconsiderable experience of envelopes they almost invariably contained news of an unfortunate nature..."

"It's a party," interrupted Pooh.

"What fun," exclaimed piglet, despite the fact that he had never been to a party and was not at all sure what one was, or is, for that matter.

"It'll rain," said Eeyore eyeing the sky with deep foreboding. "It always rains. One minute it's a beautiful sunny day then somebody mentions a party and it rains. There's no avoiding it; in my not inconsiderable experience..."

"It's inside," said Pooh. "So if it rains it won't matter."

"Ahh," said Eeyore and stared gloomily at Christopher Robin who had just arrived.

"Whose party Pooh?" he asked.

"Did someone call?" said Owl. Eeyore raised an eyebrow, realised he had put it out of reach and had to ask Kanga to get it down for him.

"It's from somebody called 'Fiff Teeith'," replied Pooh in a puzzled voice.

Christopher Robin, who was down to a bottle a day and had not touched a joint all week summoned all his patience and said, "Give it to me Silly Old Bear and let me read it."

Pooh, despite being well known as a Bear of Very Little Brain resented this unprovoked attack on his intellect and was about to say so, but something in Christopher Robin's voice persuaded him otherwise. Since Christopher Robin had joined Swampy in a tunnel protest against the felling of Hundred Acre Wood for the by-pass he had become rather unpredictable.

"It says here," said Christopher Robin, "that we are all invited to a party to celebrate Sam's 50th birthday."

"What do we wear?" asked Piglet, whose extensive wardrobe consisting entirely of identically striped T-shirts was the toast of the fashion world.

"Black Tie/Posh Frock," replied Pooh wondering whether this was a choice or a suggestion concerning cross dressing.

"Can we go?" said Piglet. "Canwecanwecanwecanwe?"

"Of course we can," replied Pooh, "just as soon as we've found Eeyore's tail."

"Will he need it then?" asked Piglet.

"No," said Pooh, "I'm going to skin it and make it into a Mohair dinner jacket."

"That's cool," said Christopher Robin as he punched in numbers on his mobile phone.

"Hey babe, just got the word on a hip scene. Some old fart just made FIFTY!! Yeah, can still walk and talk too! Might be a good piss up, wanna come?"

"What's a pressup?" inquired Piglet, who did not get out much.

"Never mind," said Pooh. "Let's go and see that nice Mr Disney and practice our mid-Atlantic accents."

"Works for me," said Piglet without having the ghost of an idea what he meant.

And so off they went.

SAM after AAM with apologies.

JUST ANOTHER TUESDAY

"Good morning," said the frog, "do sit down and make yourself comfortable."

I did as I was asked, It was not an unreasonable request, it's just that I couldn't recall having heard a frog speak before, let alone ask me to make myself comfortable.

So I sat down and attempted to arrange my thoughts.

Tuesday has always been a funny day for me. I think it started when Winnie the Pooh was identified as having trouble with the spelling. That was the watershed. Get out of bed in the morning, something strange happens; finding two Abba CDs in the microwave for instance, sure enough when you check, it's Tuesday.

Not that today had been unusual until now, but it certainly was making up for lost time I thought, as I examined my surroundings more closely. I was sitting in some kind of office. Perhaps I should explain that I didn't have the vaguest idea what I was doing here, it was of no real concern, I was just mildly curious. Facing me was a large leather-topped desk. An equally large swivel chair of the type favoured by executives and crooked financial advisers stood opposite me, and behind that was a filing cabinet where the frog (did I mention the frog? I hope so otherwise you may be having a bit of trouble grasping the point of all this) was busily searching for something.

The desk had the usual things you would expect to see on an office desk and one you would not. A photograph of two frogs, one with its arm around a smaller frog and between them a kind of bundle of shiny spherical dots. I sense you are ahead of me. Yes: frogspawn.

This was pretty bizarre even when making allowances for the day of the week. It then dawned on me that I was looking at a picture of a family group. This was but one of a number of puzzles with which I was confronted – not the least of which was that I was in the company of a very big frog, and I don't mean big in the sense of a big frog compared with others of the species. On the contrary this one was around six feet tall, which I humbly submit is a lot bigger than one would expect for your average Jeremy Fisher. This was the stuff of science fiction movies. "Attack of the Mutant Giant Frogs" springs, so to speak, to mind.

And concerning things springing to mind, my previous mild curiosity had undergone a far-reaching reappraisal. What on earth was happening? Where am I and what is going on? These questions required answers, and soon please. What if The World had been taken over by the aforementioned mutants? I'd have thought someone would have noticed. Why wasn't news of this event on the Today Programme?

Could John Humphreys be losing his grip?

Mind you I could see, looking at my frog just how they (the frogs, not The Today Programme) could have infiltrated The Establishment. It (the frog not the Establishment) was very well turned out, immaculate in hand tailored suit, crisp white shirt and perfectly centred: could it be a Regimental tie? It certainly looked like the real thing. Queens Own Amphibious Lancers perhaps? Could this be a dream? I closed my eyes, shook my head and opened my eyes again. All was as before except that the frog was now sitting, or perching or whatever frogs do on his...

His?... Suddenly I had given the green apparition in front of me a gender. I think it must have been the suit. What if it had been wearing a Vivienne Westwood dress? ANYWAY... it was now observing me from the other side of the desk.

I was just about to open the conversation with some witty and suitable repartee. The volatility of Lily Pad prices this year, for instance, or the difficulty of securing Heron free accommodation around inner city areas, when the animal suddenly tensed.

You notice things like that when facing a six-foot high, Saville Row suited Kermit look-alike. It sat completely motionless, its eyes fixed on an object on the ceiling, then without warning a long strip of green tongue darted towards the light fitting above us and lassoed an unsuspecting fly which had chosen an unfortunate, not to say fatal spot to land. The tongue returned with its prize at much the same dizzying velocity as it had been deployed and disappeared into the dark recesses of the mouth, which closed with a clearly audible "bloop".

In all honesty I have to say that it shook me up a bit. Given the size of the creature in front of me, which for all I knew was not fully-grown, I might well be on the menu as a welcome change from the common housefly.

Two bulbous eyes gazed at me across the expanse of the leather topped desk. Briefly they lowered to examine an open manila file. Then the steady unblinking discs returned to me.

The tone of voice was solicitous, even avuncular. "Ahh Mr Mummery," it said. "And how are you managing with the new drugs?"

August 31, 2001

NOTES FROM THE OPERA

I have a great fondness for things Ancient and for the Old in general. Probably because of the efforts of my Mother, amongst others, who despite her advancing years helps out in the Community and displays a capacity for work and commitment not always evident in those of less maturity.

I always try to make an effort to remember that the elders such as she have witnessed at first hand, and can recall, major events in our history, and if one can persuade them that the colour of Doris Fosdyke's dressing gown is not an essential component of the tale about the night a landmine flattened Southampton ice rink and shattered every pane of glass in the block of flats at Melbourne Terrace (or was it Sydney Avenue?) then one may be deemed fortunate to spend time with them.

And so I viewed the prospect of a visit to the local theatre to watch a production of "The Cole Porter Story" in the company of four ladies whose combined ages totalled some 320 years, with something approaching warm appreciation.

Since my car has only two doors (a deficiency regularly condemned by my Mother who is an experienced mover of the elderly and infirm and would not give such a vehicle house... er, garage room) it was decided that we would use two cars and meet at the theatre.

Due to an inexcusable lapse of concentration on my part regarding the starting time of the performance, one of the ladies and I spent a convivial forty-five minutes in conversation on a bench outside the theatre, which was in close proximity to a hostelry from which loud and repetitive "music" emanated, the lyrics of which seemed to involve something about "slapping up my bitch". We were spared any further exposure to the mysteries of recreational dog patting by the arrival of the remainder of the party.

Once inside the theatre lobby the tickets were distributed by my Mother, but not of course until a small but significant movement had been made in the group's location to ensure the creation of a bottle neck at the entrance to the stalls. We were now clearly identified as "A Group".

A tiny alarm bell rang somewhere in the back of my head; I ignored it.

Without wishing to examine in any great detail the issue of tickets and seat numbers, a discipline with which, after three decades in the Airline Industry, I am not entirely unfamiliar, the following is relevant: there were four tickets together and one apart. I elected to take the odd one and examined it. Row J seat 4. We were standing in row K. I stepped over into row J and alighted on seat 4 leaving the ladies in row K, seats 7 to 10 inclusive. I hope this is clear because it's the only explanation you are going to get.

An elderly gentleman on my left glanced at me and I greeted him with a cheery "Good Evening".

"When I booked this seat," he said, looking at me over a pair of very thick spectacles with exactly the same facial expression as I recall my Latin Master having when I translated the verb Vastare as, "to dump rubbish" (Explanation later.) "When I booked this seat," he repeated, "I was told that the view of the left hand side of the stage would not be obscured by the piano." He waved a hand in the general direction of the stage and continued. "And is that not stage left and is there not, in spite of assurances to the contrary, a piano obscuring the view?"

"Ahh, indeed there is," I confirmed, having been slightly wrong-footed by this lengthy reply to my original greeting. I would very probably at that point have launched into an automatic and enthusiastic defence of a well-known Airlines' booking and seating policy but for the interruption of a minor commotion behind us. 7 to 10 inclusive Row K were searching their handbags whilst four claimants to their seats stood over them like a malevolent cloud.

God knows, if there was anybody in the building that night who should not have assumed that 7 to 10 row K were the correct seats, it should have been me.

Having found their tickets once again in the depths of various reticules, my four companions marched out of Row K and joined me in row J, a manoeuvre that revised our identity from "a group" to "THE group".

Calm and tranquillity once more established, at least temporarily, the show began and it was soon evident that a sizeable portion of the Audience, and particularly those in the seats behind us, were enthusiastic supporters of the cast. Did Opera buffs travel with the team so to speak? Were there groupies in provincial Opera? Surely not. Something else was, regrettably, crystal clear. An unfortunate simile as it turns out. This was an Opera Company who seemed to have made an important omission in their list of prerequisites for membership.

They could not sing.

Let us try to be fair. They could sing, but rarely in the correct key when solo or in the same one *en masse.* This deficiency made the continual hurrahs and whoops from their supporters even more inappropriate since they were all, as I discovered later, hoping for parts in the next production.

When one is watching an amateur production one is obliged to allow a fairly generous margin before committing to serious criticism of the performance.

Having reached a point where the margin was so wide as to be barely visible without the use of powerful binoculars, I concluded that they really were awful. To say that they had bitten off more than they could chew fails to indicate the enormity of the task they had undertaken.

The meat, to continue the dining analogy, was very tough and whoever picked it from the butcher's window did not have a clue how to prepare it for consumption.

As the performance continued on its shaky way I began to sense a certain restlessness in my elderly companions whenever a wayward note escaped, which, as I think I have made clear, was frequently.

There was of course no audible comment, ladies of this generation being too well brought up to express their displeasure in public. Later, with the gin bottle open the entire cast will be damned in perpetuity. And if you are surprised that the preferred beverage of these gentle souls hails not from the tea leaf, but the juniper berry, do no more than look at the Queen Mother for confirmation of the powerful medicinal properties of the latter.

As yet another melody was hijacked from its composer and cruelly mutilated I became aware of a different sound drifting across the auditorium. One of my ladies was singing along with the music, and, I must add, putting the cast to shame. A further enhancement to her performance, which it took me a few moments to identify, was the extraordinary fact that her hearing aid which had been buzzing intermittently throughout the evening appeared to be in perfect harmony with her voice.

I listened and watched transfixed. It is at times like this that great ideas are conceived which at the time seem so outlandish that their chances of survival are poor, but with love and care may perhaps reach full term and burst new and resplendent into the awaiting world. I guess that on sober reflection this birth analogy is a shade melodramatic to say the least, but at the time...

Just picture the scene: The Albert Hall, a full house eagerly awaiting the first performance of a radical experiment in music. There is an air of anticipation tinged with anxiety. A thousand spectacle cases open, surrender their contents, and close again with a ripple of sound like summer rain on baked earth. The clicking of a multitude of cicadas on a hot Caribbean night assaults your senses but it is the shutting of hundreds of handbags you have heard, now clasped in bejewelled fingers and perched on countless Laura Ashley enveloped knees. In complete contrast you also witness the awesome grandeur of an Antarctic dawn. The massed choirs of elderly ladies, their blue rinses reflecting the light like a glacier snaking its slow but inexorable journey to oblivion. In the autumn of their lives a grand finale.

Bear with me whilst I regain my composure.

You are about to witness an extraordinary moment in the history of Art.

HANDEL'S MESSIAH, FROM SCRATCH, ACCOMPANIED ONLY BY NATIONAL HEALTH HEARING AIDS.

Of course it needs funding but what entrepreneur worth his venture capital could resist the challenge?

The venue is ideal, the cast eager.

There is but one detail, which troubles me in the cold sleepless hours before the dawn.

How on earth are we going to manage the seating....?

Oh yes, the Latin verb Vastare? It means "To lay waste" as in destroying a city. Well, it's a mistake anyone could make.

BUTTIES, CUTS AND STERN GLANDS

The voyage of the Narrow Boat "OMNIA" and the Trials Tribulations and Triumphs of her crew.

DAY ONE – SATURDAY

Arrive at Brewood boatyard (pronounced Brewed as in beer or brood as in er... Brood.) on time and load boat with food etc, quite a lot of etceteras as I recall. Whilst stowing his gear the cabin boy discovers that he has 23 pairs of socks but only 2 pairs underpants. On day one this does not bode well.

Weather good in the late afternoon as we leave the mooring, cabin boy is permitted to drive boat under close supervision of the Captain.

Manages to avoid damaging the vessel or anyone's mental health.

Arrive at overnight mooring, the Mermaid, Wightwick (probably pronounced Fanshaw for all I know). Convivial surroundings and excellent fayre after which we return to the boat to find that the forward door (or it might be hatch) is fitted with a dead lock which we failed to notice and so the key is useless. Several noisy and futile attempts to gain entry do not attract the attention of the local Constabulary who might, at least, have given us a place to sleep in the event of arrest for attempted burglary.

Discussion ensues concerning damage to doors, locks etc, if forced entry is attempted.

Cabin boy, whose inability to remember where he has left keys of all descriptions, has turned him into a house breaker of not inconsiderable skill persuades Captain and First Mate that a sharp blow with the boat hook on a very small pane of glass in the forward door/ hatch will cause minimal damage and get us in.

More out of desperation than confidence in the plan they agree. Cabin boy strikes small pane with aforesaid hook.

The glass fails to break but to the astonishment of all door flies open as if activated by a secret spring.

Further drama will, without doubt, follow as the trip progresses.

WEATHER: Sunny and warm, later wet and warm.

EVENT MARKER: Met a working boat with a butty in tow (unclear whether jam or chip) and saw 12 Herons sitting in a field and a fisherman spoke to us (apparently this is a rare occurrence).

DAY TWO – SUNDAY

Full English plus Champagne prepared by the Captain. Excellent. Meteorological conditions are favourable (it is dry). Under further close supervision, cabin boy driving boat enters and exits two locks without terrifying the local populace.

Lunch at the Wagon and horses near a bridge. Not sure why bridge is significant other than to distinguish it from another pub of the same name on the canal and frankly don't care much either.

Back on the cut the afternoon weather deteriorates rapidly. Several breeds of dogs and cats identified.

Also identify Homosapiens hunting aquatic prey with rod and line. At a guess 100 plus of these hardy souls in full waterproofs and surrounded by tackle. Similarly clad and standing on the stern of a narrow boat open to the elements, the crew of Omnia. Should either of these groups be seeking psychiatric help? Discuss...

The itinery states, "Water at Greensforge Lock". Quite a lot of water elsewhere too...

Arrive Stourton Junction, moist but undaunted.

After "mooring up", an expression which describes tying each end of the boat to the canal bank with string, the cabin boy is introduced to the tradition of greasing the stern gland, which he needn't have worried about after all.

Dinner on board prepared by first mate. The stew type dish was very tasty despite being described by its creator as "looking like slurry" which, given the proximity of the mooring to a pig farm was an unfortunate phrase.

WEATHER: As stated or worse.

EVENT MARKER: 22.00 Rain ceased 22.03 Rain returned.

WEED HATCH INVENTORY: Weed.

DAY THREE – MONDAY

Early start after unexpected hurricane. Michael Fish not involved. No damage except to sleep patterns caused by anxiety as to whether narrow boats are designed to resist the impact of falling oak trees.

Bright morning, with hurricane now downgraded to stiff breeze.

Omnia casts off at 07.35. Enters first lock 07.37. Clears first lock 07.45.

Cabin boy traumatised by early lock duty. Lies down for an hour.

Only 27 more locks to do today. 4 at Stourton Junction. The Stourbridge 16 (freed on appeal) and the very picturesque Delph Flight with 7 to climb.

At number 5 on the Delph a very big (not to say enormous, because one does not want to be accused of exaggeration) rat, runs over the cabin boy's foot and cowers at the lock gate. Cabin boy rooted to the spot with concern for the animal, which is evidently not in the best of health.

The Captain dispatches the rodent as humanly as possible with a backhand smash, a stroke difficult enough with a tennis racquet, never mind a windlass, which is the only item of sports equipment available.

Clear all locks in dry weather despite threatening sky. Captain very nearly scores max points on timing arrival in Birmingham but is thwarted by vigorous line squall which strikes as we are tying up. Cabin boy who is not trained to secure boat and erect umbrella simultaneously, gets wet, so does First Mate who is trained but lacks umbrella.

Following light lunch entire crew locate shopping mall to purchase essential stores. Cabin boy goes in search of underwear and cash machine. Finds former but not latter.

First Mate has completed essential stores acquisition (wine gums and liquorice allsorts), all return to vessel.

Cabin boy driving, copes admirably with first 300 yards then runs aground whilst avoiding traffic.

Captain restores boat to deeper water. Rest of afternoon passes without major incident other than unfortunate confusion over bow and stern whilst manoeuvring at water pick up point, and badly judged turn through narrow bridge nearly resulting in spillage of Captain's and First Mate's sloe gin (a capital offence I understand).

Further disappointment after mooring at Windmill End close to pub famous for "Desperate Dan Cow Pie". No food tonight due to snow on the points at Didcot, or other feeble excuse. Try pub next door, similar lack of sustenance. Note: Do not plan to eat out on a Monday in Dudley (Pronounced Dud Lie).

Eat aboard to accompaniment of 60s hits and copious quantities of claret.

WEATHER: Dry with damp patches.

EVENT MARKER: Cabin boy grounds boat, spills sloe gin.

WEED HATCH INVENTORY: One pair ladies black knickers, one traffic cone.

DAY FOUR – TUESDAY

Hurricane superseded by Monsoon last night. Several drowned rats sighted.

Leisurely breakfast of boiled eggs prepared by Cabin boy. Nobody died.

First treat of the day, The Netherton Tunnel, 3027metres in length. The last canal tunnel to be dug in Britain it was completed in 1858. By that time the writing was on the walls for the canals and this was a last ditch effort (sorry, couldn't resist it) to compete with the railways.

When completed it boasted towpaths on both sides and was gas lit from end to end.

A quite amazing feat of engineering it also has remarkable acoustic qualities, a property utilised in full by the Captain whose rendition of some of the louder ballads and songs of the cut added a degree of authenticity to the passage so early in the morning...

Omnia leaves the tunnel reverberating to the last chorus of a song concerned with living conditions on the cut, the scarcity of work and general gloom about the future of mankind, and joins a stretch called the Birmingham Main Line. There is now another main line next to it, this one providing navigation for railway locomotives.

Our planned visit to the Black Country Museum is enhanced by the news that since we are in a narrow boat we may moor and stay overnight within the grounds of the museum. For reasons which were not entirely clear and were probably highly technical it was deemed prudent to turn the boat around before mooring. This manoeveure was executed by the Captain in front of a sizeable crowd of onlookers. The cabin boy who was "in charge front end string" stood, a line dangling nonchalantly from his hand trying to look as if the crew did this sort of thing nightly and matinees Tuesday and Thursday, as the prow passed through 180 degrees and never less or more than 6 inches from the bank. Were they impressed? You bet, and they were not alone in their admiration.

The living history of the Black Country museum deserves much more than a passing reference but it is not within the scope of this log other than to say if you haven't visited, put it at the top of your recreational list... You don't have one? Well it's high time you did. See to it as a matter of urgency please.

In the golden glow of an autumn evening the crew sink a couple of glasses of a similarly tinted beverage and then it's off to the sophisticated and genteel dining experience to be had at Mad O'Rourke's Pie House, namely Desperate Dan Cow Pie.

WEATHER: Dry and Warm.

EVENT MARKER: Local youths attempt to burn down a concrete bridge and seem surprised to note that their endeavour is not crowned with success. It is quite clear that physics needs to be given a much higher priority within the British Educational System.

WEED HATCH INVENTORY: Forgot to look.

DAY FIVE – WEDNESDAY

Leisurely breakfast then off to Wolverhampton where the cabin boy will jump ship due to a pressing engagement at home.

Is given the helm with the news that there are no locks on this stretch.

It is true there are no locks but there is a plentiful supply of narrow twisting stretches with bridges and a tunnel. Cabin boy is coping well with narrow twisting etc, when, on a blind turn plus bridge, crosswind, plagues of locusts and a heavy swell... ANOTHER boat appears. Not only a boat but a huge (not to say enormous) barge in tow containing a number of people who look as if they are about to start work on a Ground force project.

Cabin boy stated later that the accusation of blind panic from the Captain was grossly unfair. He had both eyes open, a clear indication that he was only half blind and the collision risk was on his good side so he was aware of the conflict. The profane outburst of which he was accused was an attempt to alert the Captain to a situation, which he felt fell outside his area of competence.

Swift intervention by the Captain averts disaster and as Wolverhampton and its DSMs (Dark Satanic Mills) looms close the cabin boy relinquishes the helm to prepare for his journey home by rail, poignantly, the transport system that heralded an end to the dominance of the canal network.

For the cabin boy amidst a kaleidoscope of images, one defines Narrow Boating in its entirety.

It is the elderly gentleman enjoying his morning stroll along the towpath offering a cheery greeting as he overtakes the cruising boat.

October 21, 2001

SWANS

I watched them as they turned toward the lake, their wings blindingly white in the afternoon sunshine. "Look," I called to her, "look at the swans." She slipped her hand into mine. I loved the way she did that. She could make it feel like a very special moment, as if it had never happened before.

We stood silently watching the great birds as slowly they descended, the cob slightly ahead of his mate, she following his every move, so close that it seemed some invisible bond must join them. As close as the golden down on the back of her neck... As close as the hint of her perfume on the breeze...

I remember when sometimes we were going out to eat with friends and were about to leave the house she would hang behind, grab me and kiss me, hard and urgently, then dance away from me with a big grin and whisper, "Later, don't be so impatient..."

The birds touched down leaving a silvery wake in the still water tiny ripples moving out and back tracing their movement. We watched them drift across the water still so close their feathers seemed to be entwined.

Then something extraordinary happened, the cob turned slightly towards his mate and stroked her neck with his beak. It was a gesture of pure affection and she responded lifting her head and turning to meet his caress, for that was indeed the only way to describe it. I was about to say something but she squeezed my hand stopped me from ruining the moment. We gazed at them for what seemed an age until they disappeared from view.

She looked at me, sparkling ice blue eyes, and the ghost of a smile. "Take me home now and love me like that." Her voice was soft but firm.

She moved slowly toward me. She wore one of my shirts, nothing else.

I reached for her and stroked her neck, she closed her eyes I moved my hand down to undo the one button she had fastened, fascinated by the outline of her breasts against the fabric, and gently slid the shirt of her shoulders as I had done many times before. But this afternoon was different, as if it was the first time all over again.

The shirt turned into a puddle of white cotton at her feet. She lifted her head and looked straight into my eyes, she was simply exquisite. I held her close, running my fingers down the curve of her back, kissing her neck and shoulders. She wrapped a long smooth leg round me and pulled me close. Then suddenly we were one tumbling, stroking, writhing mass of desire.

The taste and smell of her was intoxicating, I was embarking on a journey with no destination from which I never wanted to return, and we loved. Oh! How we loved with a burning intensity, which I should have known, heralded the end.

I remember one hot afternoon lying beside her listening to her steady breathing, knowing she was asleep. She had one hand on my forearm and as I lifted myself on an elbow to look at her, the contact was briefly broken. She immediately moved her hand to find me but her steady breathing did not change. Her face had a child like quality when she slept and I felt a great need to protect her, quite from what I was not entirely sure. I gazed in real wonder at her body, each smooth flowing curve complementing the next and at her long slender legs which earlier had held me with surprising strength. Her eyes opened.

"What are you looking at you dirty old man?" she teased.

"An angel," I replied.

She ran a hand through my hair, "Not quite," she said and for a moment she was a long way away...

Later we lay like spoons; drifting in and out of sleep.

"They mate for life," she said very softly.

"Who does?" I replied, not really paying attention.

"Swans," she repeated. "They mate for life and if one dies the other will pine and sometimes dies too."

Her tone of voice had changed. I had a terrible sense of foreboding, she turned to face me; tears streamed down her cheeks like tiny liquid diamonds.

"I can't do this anymore," she said. "I'm sorry."

"The swans reminded you," I said flatly.

"Yes."

There was nothing more to say.

We clung to each other in a last embrace, but the spell was broken. The afternoon sun turned to twilight a time when all lunchtime lovers know they must part.

I return to the lake from time to time but I am pretty sure that our pair have not been back. I hope they are still together somewhere and I also wonder whether the beautiful girl who brightened my life, however briefly, sometimes looks at the lake and remembers the day when our love was touched by the magic and intensity of the wild.

December 10, 2001